BAKE IT OFF

BAKE IT OFF

An Unofficial Taylor Swift–Inspired Cookbook for Every Era, from Breakfast to *Midnights*

LINDSEY SMITH

Recipes by Kristin Richards

This book is not affiliated with and has not been authorized, licensed, or endorsed by Taylor Swift.

Without limiting the exclusive rights of any author, contributor or the publisher of this publication, any unauthorized use of this publication to train generative artificial intelligence (AI) technologies is expressly prohibited. HarperCollins also exercise their rights under Article 4(3) of the Digital Single Market Directive 2019/790 and expressly reserve this publication from the text and data mining exception.

The material on linked sites referenced in this book is the author's own. HarperCollins disclaims all liability that may result from the use of the material contained at those sites. All such material is supplemental and not part of the book. The author reserves the right to close the website in her sole discretion at any time.

BAKE IT OFF. Copyright © 2025 by Lindsey Smith. All rights reserved. Printed in Canada. No part of this book may be used or reproduced in any manner whatsoever without written permission except in the case of brief quotations embodied in critical articles and reviews. For information, address HarperCollins Publishers, 195 Broadway, New York, NY 10007. In Europe, HarperCollins Publishers, Macken House, 39/40 Mayor Street Upper, Dublin 1, D01 C9W8, Ireland.

HarperCollins books may be purchased for educational, business, or sales promotional use. For information, please email the Special Markets Department at SPsales@harpercollins.com.

hc.com

FIRST EDITION

Designed by Tai Blanche
Photography by Jak Kerley
Pink glitter texture and sky backgrounds © stock.adobe.com

Library of Congress Cataloging-in-Publication Data has been applied for.

ISBN 978-0-06-345015-8

25 26 27 28 29 TC 10 9 8 7 6 5 4 3 2 1

To Swifties—old and new.
I love fighting dragons with you.

lovelovelove
-L-

CONTENTS

Introduction: Hey, Hey, Hey! 1

Bonus: Kitty Cakes and Dog Bones 204

Acknowledgments 206

Easter Egg Key 207

Universal Conversion Chart 210

Index 211

Breakfast at Midnight 32
Sweet Treats Perfect for Breakfast . . . or *Midnights*

Karma Is a Cookie 58
Cookies, Cookies, and More Cookies!

I Bet You Think About Cake 94
Cakes, Cupcakes, and Bars

Pie, Pie, Baby! 122
Pies, Tarts, and Other Doughy Treats

Pastries That Look Like Dresses 154
Danishes, Croissants, Pretzels, and Other Pastries

Junior Jewels 480
Candies and Other Confections

INTRODUCTION

Hey, Hey, Hey!

Welcome to *Bake It Off*—the unofficial and unauthorized cookbook for Swifties by Swifties.

Whether you are an OG Swiftie from the days of Myspace, a newly anointed Tortured Poet, or someone who just loves baking for friends and family, there is a little sweet something in this baking book for everyone to enjoy. And at this table, we'll save you a seat.

Bake It Off includes 50-plus Taylor-inspired recipes representing each and every era. This book spans the country days of Taylor's self-titled debut album and her transition to pop stardom all the way to the cabin vibes of *folklore* and *evermore* and on to *The Tortured Poets Department*. From cakes to cookies to candies prepared in cardigans, each is uniquely infused with a style and taste that will leave the crowd chanting "MORE!"

To ensure that no member of your squad is left out, there are also plenty of vegan, gluten-free, and nut-free treats. After all, Taylor is known for her generous spirit—a pop star who makes homemade Pop-Tarts for the Kansas City Chiefs and who donated to food banks in each city of the Eras Tour, she is the definition of a caring queen who rises to every occasion.

You don't have to be a fourteen-time Grammy Award winner to enjoy these delights, but you'll probably feel like one after tasting treats like Illicit Éclairs (page 163), Cowboy (Cookies) Like Me (page 60), or The Best Day(nish) (page 156).

Like any good creation (whether it's music or baked goods), it's meant to be shared. You can gift your creations to a friend or neighbor, bring a batch of cookies to a Super Bowl party, or even host a *Bake It Off* par-tay (see page 10) and invite your squad over for an afternoon or evening of music and baking together (friendship bracelet trading optional).

However you decide to bake it off, I hope you'll remember the moments made sharing these confections with the ones you love the most.

Journey to Swifties

It was a typical Tuesday night in June 2006. I had just graduated from high school a few weeks earlier and was getting ready for my first year at college.

I was driving shotgun with my best friend, Ashley, on the back roads of my small Pennsylvania town when a new artist hit the radio waves. It was Taylor Swift, whose first single, "Tim McGraw," had just launched.

While I wasn't typically a country fan, I was obsessed with this song and thought it was super clever to write a song named after a country singer. While she released several singles off her debut album, it was "Picture to Burn" that turned me from casual radio listener to full-on Swiftie, and I couldn't wait to get my hands on the album. I loved the angst and how Taylor was unapologetically being herself.

I remember buying the *Fearless* CD when it first came out and driving around in my gold Saturn belting out "You Belong with Me" and "Love Story." I watched the music videos religiously. I read the liner notes for Easter eggs. When her documentary series *Journey to Fearless* aired on TV, I canceled all my plans so I could tune in weekly. (And, yes, I cried while watching it then and I cried rewatching it years later.)

In a weird way, I feel like we grew up together. After all, we are around the same age and both grew up in small Pennsylvania towns. When she was struggling to make friends, so was I. When she found solace in her one best friend, Abigail, I found solace in my one best friend, Ashley. When I was going through a breakup, I would belt "All Too Well" and cry. It was like every emotion she was experiencing, I at some point was, too. I loved watching every interview of hers, every social media post, and, of course, her performances.

In July 2013, I had the opportunity to work the perfume booth at the Red Tour in Pittsburgh and got to stay for the entire show. Even though I was by myself, it was like I was in a room full of friends and the host, Taylor Swift, was getting ready to greet us. Her concerts have always been a safe space for me, evenings where a group of strangers who felt like friends could be free to be themselves and experience nothing but pure joy.

When I came up with the idea of *Bake It Off*, I wanted to lean in all the way and infuse all I love about Taylor and her work in a way that would make it fun for fellow Swifties, not just through the recipes alone but also through the Easter eggs in the text and photos. (Like Taylor, I had to keep spreadsheets of Easter eggs just for this project.)

Since I am a home baker and not a professional baker, I knew I needed to find a fellow Swiftie to help elevate these recipes to the fullest. So I tagged in fellow

Pennsylvanian and newly anointed Swiftie, Kristen Richards. Kristen is a baker and the owner of Front Porch Baking Co. in Millersville, Pennsylvania. After eating her amazing treats for years, I knew she was the ~~man~~ woman for the job. Kristen is a new Swiftie, someone who has been a casual listener over the years but who really grew to appreciate her in the *folklore*, *evermore*, *Midnights*, and *Tortured Poets Department* eras. You can now hear Taylor's discography in full rotation if you visit Kristen's bakery.

    Whether your journey to Swiftie stems way back to the Myspace days or it's just beginning today, at this table (hopefully now full of delicious baked goods), everyone is welcome.

lovelovelove,

—S

. . . Ready for It? Getting Started in the Kitchen

Dear Baker: Wash your hands clean and let's dive into some basics before you start to bake it off. There *are* rules here, especially when it comes to baking, and this section includes some tips to help you get started with ease.

Read the liner notes: Before starting a recipe, it's best to first read the entire recipe. If you don't, you might get a few steps in and realize you don't have what you need or did something in the wrong order and need to begin again. Reading the recipe beforehand helps ensure that you are completely prepared. Think of this as a dress rehearsal before the big show!

The right place at the right time: In the culinary world, this is called mise en place. It helps you say "je suis calme" before you begin. Measuring all your ingredients and arranging all your tools beforehand will help you move through the creation process with confidence. It's kind of like having your lyrics, samples, and notes organized before heading to the studio to record.

Don't be afraid to jump, then fall: If you are new to baking, it can take some practice to get it right. After all, you don't just become a global star overnight. This comes from years of practice and hard work. There are also factors that can be a bit outside of your control—like varying oven temperatures and things like *mean* humidity that can cause a recipe to be slightly off. It's okay to make mistakes. You can shake it off and try again.

Long live confetti sprinkles and edible glitter: While not every single recipe has confetti sprinkles or edible glitter, feel free to decorate your creations in any way that makes you feel enchanted. Also, is there such a thing as too much glitter?

Have fun with special dates: We all know that Taylor loves her numerology. Whether it's April 29, July 9, or December 13, there is always a reason or day to celebrate with pastries and baked goods. When those special occasions come around, choose a recipe from *Bake It Off* to make and celebrate!

Share with your squad: While pastries and baked goods can definitely be consumed while you are home alone with your cats, they are also fun when shared with friends. You could even have a *Bake It Off* par-tay and invite your squad over for an evening of baking and making fun of your exes.

Be yourself: As Taylor Swift once said, "If they don't like you for being yourself, be yourself even more." Lean in to your likes and tastes when making recipes, and don't be afraid to swap a flavor or ingredient for something you like even more. Just like Taylor encourages us to make her songs our own, we encourage you to make these recipes your own!

Baking Tools

While Taylor's tools include a guitar, picks, microphones, and sequined dresses, bakers require specialty tools like pastry bags, specific pans, cookie cutters, and aprons. (Aprons may be less sparkly, but they can still be really fun!)

For most recipes, you just need the basics. However, there are some recipes that call for a few specialty items. As you build your baking muscles, these are some items you might want to add to your arsenal of tools.

The Basics

These are some of the must-haves to get started baking many of the treats in this book. Think of this section as your guitar pick and guitar.

Mixing bowls: Having a variety of bowl sizes on hand for various baking projects can help you prepare all your ingredients ahead of time for easier execution of the recipe.

Measuring cups and spoons: Since much of baking is precise measurements, it's crucial to have measuring cups and spoons for both liquid and dry ingredients.

Baking sheets: Flat baking sheets are perfect for baking cookies and making sheet cakes and can be easily transferred from countertop to freezer.

Spatulas: Flexible silicone spatulas in an assortment of sizes are ideal for scraping mixing bowls, folding in ingredients, and spreading batters.

Whisk: A whisk helps eliminate lumps in batters and creams and can add air to your mixture.

Wooden spoons: Wooden spoons come in handy for mixing thicker doughs and batters.

Cake pans: Cake pans come in a variety of sizes and shapes—round, square, and rectangle. Perfect for cakes, bars, Rice Krispies treats, and more.

Loaf pans: These pans are essential for making breads, pound cakes, and other loaf-style recipes.

Pie dishes: Used for pies and quiches, these dishes come in a variety of depths.

Muffin tins: These tins are your go-to for cupcakes, muffins, mini pies, tarts, and quiches.

Wire cooling racks: These racks help baked goods cool evenly.

Parchment paper: This is probably my most-used tool in the kitchen. It keeps pans mess-free and makes cleanup a breeze.

Rolling pin: This tool is helpful for rolling out dough for piecrusts and cookies. No rolling pin? No problem. A bottle of priceless (or cheap!) wine or olive oil will do.

Sifter: Sometimes dry ingredients like flour or confectioners' sugar must be sifted to ensure a lump-free mixture. Although you can alternatively sift using a fine-mesh sieve, a sifter makes this task a cinch.

Hand mixer: A hand mixer can greatly speed up the mixing process and ensure that you have even and smooth batters. A stand mixer is also a good choice.

Food processor: A food processor can simplify tasks such as grinding nuts and cutting butter into flour.

Specialty Items

These specialty items are not necessarily needed every day, but on occasion they come in handy. Think of when Taylor performs with a twelve-string or Koi fish guitar. She could use them for every song, but she chooses to reserve them for special events or specific songs.

Bundt cake pan: This specialty pan with a tube shape and fluted edges is perfect for making coffee cakes or pound cakes.

Candy thermometer: This tool helps monitor the heat when you make candy, such as caramel and fudge, so that you can ensure your treats achieve the proper consistency.

Madeleine mold: Madeleines, the iconic seashell-shaped cookies (which are actually cakes), get their shape from the unique impressions in this mold.

Tart pans: Tart pans are shallow baking pans with fluted sides. Individual pans are commonly found in 9 to 11 inches, but small single-serving tarts can be made in mini tart pans, which are slightly larger than a muffin tin.

Popsicle molds: These molds come in a variety of shapes and sizes, and some have reusable handles. We recommend a jewel-shape mold for our Arcade Ring Popsicles (page 184), but you can choose any shape that makes you happy.

Piping bags and tips: These bags and tips are used to decorate cakes and cupcakes, fill pastries, and add decorative elements to desserts. Flower and star tips make decorating easy and fun.

Springform pan: A springform pan is a round baking pan with removable sides, which allows a delicate baked good—think cheesecake, tart, or layered desserts—to be released without having to flip it.

Cookie scoops: Spring-loaded scoops come in a variety of sizes and give your cookies a uniform size and shape. (Not just for sweets, the scoop can be used for meatballs, too.)

Spice grinder: This tool is designed to finely grind whole spices, herbs, and seeds to a powder to help enhance the flavors.

Colorful Add-Ons

When in doubt, add color. If you are looking for a way to enhance, brighten, or bejewel your baking creations, here are some of the best ingredients to have on hand.

Cookie cutters: Stars, hearts, sunglasses, moons, Saturns. There are so many cookie cutters that give us Swiftie vibes. Start small and build your collection!

Sprinkles: Sprinkles are the best way to add a confetti look or pop to any treat. When in doubt, sprinkles make everything more fun. Plus, they come in a variety of sizes, shapes, and colors, so you can customize for themes, sports teams, or holidays.

Candy melts: Candy melts are a sugar coating designed to melt quickly, making them perfect for dipping and decorating treats. They come in a wide variety of colors and several flavors. You can use them to dip marshmallows, pretzels, and fruit, or you can place them in molds if you want a certain shape or look. They are an easy way to add a pop of color to almost any treat.

Food dyes: Food dyes come in liquid, gel, and powdered forms. Along with natural food coloring, the dyes can enhance the colors of batters, frostings, and chocolate molds.

Edible glitter: If you want to make your whole plate of baked goods shimmer, add edible glitter. There is glitter dust, flaky glitter (like gold), and gel or spray glitter. They add a little sparkle to cakes, cupcakes, cookies, drinks, and chocolates and other candies. You can enhance almost any pastry with a little extra sparkle.

Edible pens and writing gel: Gel pens, fountain pens, quill pens, and now edible pens and writing gel for baking are perfect for writing your favorite lyric or "Happy Birthday!" on a cookie or cake.

Isomalt: Isomalt is a glass-like sugar used in making decorative pieces like edible gemstones, candies, sculptures, or windowpanes in cookies or pastries. In Invisible Locket Shaker Cookies (page 75), it provides a visible window for viewing the sprinkles on the inside of the cookie.

Can You Spot the Easter Eggs?

One of the things that I've always loved about Taylor is her notorious Easter eggs. She's been dropping them as early as her debut album. I remember obsessively reading her liner notes, trying to decode the secret messages she was leaving. I would scribble the message I got on a piece of paper and message my friends to see if they got the same one. It didn't take long before I was fully down the rabbit hole, and, honestly, it's been a really good time. It's one of my favorite things about being a Swiftie.

    Because of my love of Easter eggs, I wanted to make them a big part of this book. From nods to songs in the recipe titles and headnotes to subtle (and not so subtle) visuals in the photos, every recipe contains at least one Easter egg—and some have multiples. Some of these eggs are very in your face, whereas others might be deep cuts. One of the most fun parts about making this book was not even realizing that some of my Easter eggs were Easter eggs until after the fact. I would often scream, *"OMG, we got another one!"*

    If you want to go down the rabbit hole, this is your chance to dive in deep with us! (We promise, this is a rabbit hole you will survive and might even have a little fun with!)

    If you find an Easter egg, post about it with the hashtag #bakeitoff. Who knows? Maybe you'll find ones that even we missed! There is also a key at the back of the book (page 207) if you need some hints.

Host a *Bake It Off* Par-Tay

Whether it's your birthday, Taylor's birthday, or a typical Tuesday night, there is always a reason to celebrate. And what better way to celebrate than with some baked goods and your best pals?

This section provides you with some helpful tips for hosting a chill movie night in, a competitive game night, an album-release celebration, or any other par-tay you desire. And if there is glitter on the floor after the par-tay, you know you did it right.

Ways to Bake It Off

When deciding what your par-tay theme will be, you need to figure out if you will be supplying the goods, if each guest will be bringing something, or if you'll be making the goods together.

The host makes the baked goods: If the host wants to supply the baked goods ahead of time, decide what recipes you want to make. Lean in to one era or expand to multiple eras.

Each guest brings a different era: Hosting a large par-tay? Have each guest bring a recipe from a different era. Bonus points if they decorate it or make an entire theme based on the era.

Bake together: Baking one recipe together is another fun par-tay approach. Each guest can bring a different ingredient, or the host can supply everything. Invisible Locket Shaker Cookies (page 75), a recipe with multiple steps, is ideal for a group baking experience.

Enjoy a *Bake It Off* competition: Baby, let the games begin! Consider choosing a few recipes and making a competition out of it. Give prizes for things like best tasting and most stylish.

Do a combo of the above: When it comes to throwing a par-tay, the options are endless. The biggest thing is that you have fun, enjoy treats, and spend quality time with people you love.

Types of Par-Tays

Of course, there are many reasons to celebrate all year long, but here are some special ways to celebrate in true Swiftie style.

Make it a special date: There are 365 days to celebrate in a year, but for Swifties, there are meaningful dates that give us an extra reason to celebrate. Here are a few to add to your rotation of celebrations:

- July 9
- April 29
- The Fourth of July
- Anniversaries of album releases
- Upcoming album-release dates (duh!)
- Taylor's birthday: Make December 13 a national holiday for you and your friends and host a Taylor Birthday ParTay complete with cake, beverages, and special playlists. End the evening with a toast to your real friends!

Host a movie night: Make a batch of the Rep Going Down Popcorn (page 197), queue up *Taylor Swift: The Eras Tour* on the big screen, and sing along with your favorite people.

Let the games begin night: Feeling a bit competitive? Host a game night playing your favorite board games, like Scrabble or Uno. Or if you want to show off your own star power, host a karaoke contest where each guest performs their favorite Taylor song. Bonus points for costumes and choreography.

Host a T Party: Is brunch more your style? Host a T Party, complete with tea, coffee, and baked goods. This is reminiscent of the parties Taylor used to host; she'd invite fans after her shows to enjoy pizza, baked goods, games, and, of course, meeting Taylor and taking photos. Even though Taylor might not be able to make it to your T Party, she will be there in spirit.

Other Ways to Bejewel Your Par-Tay

Friendship bracelet station: To commemorate the evening, set up a station to make and swap friendship bracelets with your best pals.

Par-tay favors: If you want to leave your guests with something extra special, make a par-tay favor. You can make a custom friendship bracelet that commemorates the evening, lean in to the era or eras the party is centered around, or create a gift bag of some of your favorite Taylor-coded items like red heart-shaped sunglasses, snake rings, glitter pens, or a mini bottle of champagne.

Take-away tins: Encourage your friends to take treats home by providing a tin (heart shape optional) to go home with.

Instant camera photo booth: Set up a photo booth area and take instant pics with you and your friends all night. Label your photos with the date on the bottom so all your friends will leave with a memento of a fun evening.

See the lights, the party, the ball gowns: Hat tip to the theme of the par-tay by dressing up from your favorite era. Go comfy with the PJ set from the "You Belong with Me" music video or dress in a full ball gown from "Love Story." Take it a step further and give out a Tay-rophy to the best costume of the evening.

Create a par-tay playlist: Curate your own special par-tay playlist, or use one provided in the book. Bonus points if you create a special one that includes every song Taylor sings about parties.

Bake It Off Playlists

We can all agree that no one has better timing than Taylor—and that includes in the kitchen. No need to be taken out of the flow by a loud beep or buzz.

Instead, listen to a few Taylor tracks that are roughly the same length as the baking time listed, then enjoy a fresh-baked treat. Best. Encore. Ever.

We've categorized these playlists by typical (and approximate) baking times throughout the book and feature playlists from each album (Taylor's Versions only, of course) and a special eras mash-up.

Don't feel like adding to your list? We built custom playlists in Spotify for you. Simply use the QR code on the left, pick a baking time, and press play. Easy as pie.

Playlists by Baking Time, Album, and the Eras Tour Surprise Song Mash-Up

8 MINUTES

Taylor Swift: "Tied Together with a Smile," "Stay Beautiful"
Fearless: "Fearless," "Mr. Perfectly Fine" (From the Vault)
Speak Now: "Speak Now," "Haunted"
Red: "Red," "State of Grace"
1989: "Style," "Welcome to New York"
Reputation: "End Game" (ft. Ed Sheeran and Future), "Delicate"
Lover: "I Forgot That You Existed," "Cornelia Street"
folklore: "Cardigan," "Seven"
evermore: "Willow," "Cowboy Like Me"
Midnights: "The Great War," "Labyrinth"
The Tortured Poets Department: "Guilty as Sin?," "The Smallest Man Who Ever Lived"
The Eras Tour Surprise Song Mash-Up: "Tim McGraw," "Mirrorball"

10 MINUTES

Taylor Swift: "A Place in This World," "The Outside," "Our Song"
Fearless: "You Belong with Me," "That's When" (From the Vault), "Love Story"
Speak Now: "Back to December," "Timeless" (From the Vault)
Red: "All Too Well" (10-Minute Version—duh!)
1989: "Blank Space," "Shake It Off," "Slut!"
Reputation: ". . . Ready for It?," "Getaway Car," "Call It What You Want"
Lover: "Cruel Summer," "The Archer," "Paper Rings"
folklore : "The 1," "Illicit Affairs," "Hoax"
evermore: "Gold Rush," "Ivy," "Closure"
Midnights: "Maroon," "You're on Your Own, Kid," "Dear Reader"
The Tortured Poets Department: "Who's Afraid of Little Old Me?," "Peter"
The Eras Tour Surprise Song Mash-Up: "Fifteen," "Cornelia Street"

12 MINUTES

Taylor Swift: "Tim McGraw," "Should've Said No," "Tied Together with a Smile"
Fearless: "The Best Day," "Bye Bye Baby" (From the Vault), "White Horse"
Speak Now: "Mine," "The Story of Us," "Mean"
Red: "Stay Stay Stay," "Sad Beautiful Tragic," "22"
1989: "Out of the Woods," "I Know Places," "This Love"
Reputation: "I Did Something Bad," "Don't Blame Me," "King of My Heart"
Lover: "I Think He Knows," "Cornelia Street," "Death by a Thousand Cuts"
folklore: "Mirrorball," "Invisible String," "Epiphany"
evermore: "Champagne Problems," "No Body, No Crime (ft. HAIM)," "Coney Island" (ft. The National)
Midnights: "Mastermind," "Paris," "Midnight Rain," "Karma"
The Tortured Poets Department: "Cassandra," "The Prophecy," "How Did It End?"
The Eras Tour Surprise Song Mash-Up: "I Almost Do," "Gorgeous," "Hey Stephen"

15 MINUTES

Taylor Swift: "Teardrops on My Guitar," "Cold as You," "Mary's Song (Oh My My My)," "Should've Said No"

Fearless: "Fifteen," "Untouchable," "Change"

Speak Now: "Enchanted," "Back to December," "Innocent"

Red: "I Knew You Were Trouble," "Begin Again," "The Very First Night" (From the Vault), "Treacherous"

1989: "All You Had to Do Was Stay," "Clean," "Bad Blood (ft. Kendrick Lamar)," "Say Don't Go"

Reputation: "Gorgeous," "I Did Something Bad," "Dress," "Delicate"

Lover: "Lover," "Afterglow," "Cruel Summer," "Daylight"

folklore: "The Last Great American Dynasty," "August," "This Is Me Trying," "Peace"

evermore: "Willow," "Happiness," "Dorothea," "Closure"

Midnights: "Anti-Hero," "Snow on the Beach," "Maroon," "Labyrinth"

The Tortured Poets Department: "The Tortured Poets Department," "But Daddy I Love Him," "thanK you aIMee"

The Eras Tour Surprise Song Mash-Up: "The Last Time," "State of Grace," "Daylight"

18 MINUTES

Taylor Swift: "Our Song," "The Outside," "Stay Beautiful," "Teardrops on My Guitar," "A Place in This World"

Fearless: "Breathe," "You're Not Sorry," "Forever & Always" (Piano Version), "Fearless"

Speak Now: "Long Live," "Sparks Fly," "Better Than Revenge," "When Emma Falls in Love" (From the Vault)

Red: "Treacherous," "Everything Has Changed," "Forever Winter" (From the Vault), "All Too Well"

1989: "Welcome to New York," "Out of the Woods," "Is It Over Now?," "How You Get the Girl," "Now That We Don't Talk"

Reputation: "... Ready For It?," "Call It What You Want," "This is Why We Can't Have Nice Things," "End Game" (ft. Ed Sheeran & Future), "Gorgeous"
Lover: "I Forgot That You Existed," "The Archer," "Miss Americana & the Heartbreak Prince," "Paper Rings," "Cornelia Street"
folklore: "Exile" (ft. Bon Iver), "My Tears Ricochet," "Betty," "The 1"
evermore: "Champagne Problems," "evermore" (ft. Bon Iver), "Long Story Short," "Cowboy Like Me"
Midnights: "The Great War," "Mastermind," "Maroon," "Bejeweled," "High Infidelity"
The Tortured Poets Department: "Down Bad," "So Long, London," "I Can Fix Him (No Really I Can)," "I Can Do It with a Broken Heart," "Fortnight" (ft. Post Malone)
The Eras Tour Surprise Song Mash-Up: "I Know Places," "Red," "Call It What You Want," "Treacherous," "You're on Your Own, Kid"

22 MINUTES
Taylor Swift: "Cold as You," "Tied Together with a Smile," "Should've Said No," "Picture to Burn," "Our Song," "Mary's Song (Oh My My My)"
Fearless: "The Way I Loved You," "Mr. Perfectly Fine" (From the Vault), "Fifteen," "You Belong with Me," "Bye Bye Baby" (From the Vault)
Speak Now: "Dear John," "Haunted," "Superman," "Last Kiss"
Red: "22," "The Last Time," "Sad Beautiful Tragic," "I Almost Do," "Message in a Bottle" (From the Vault)
1989: "Shake It Off," "You Are in Love," "Bad Blood," "Suburban Legends," "Blank Space," "Slut!"
Reputation: "Look What You Made Me Do," "Delicate," "Don't Blame Me," "Getaway Car," "King of My Heart," "New Year's Day"
Lover: "You Need to Calm Down," "I Think He Knows," "Death by a Thousand Cuts," "London Boy," "Lover," "I Forgot That You Existed," "It's Nice to Have a Friend"

folklore: "Cardigan," "Mirrorball," "Illicit Affairs," "Seven," "This Is Me Trying," "Peace"

evermore: "Gold Rush," "Dorothea," "Champagne Problems," "Ivy," "Closure," "Willow"

Midnights: "Lavender Haze," "You're on Your Own, Kid," "Karma," "Dear Reader," "Paris," "Sweet Nothing," "Vigilante Shit"

The Tortured Poets Department: "The Black Dog," "Clara Bow," "Florida!!!" (ft. Florence and the Machine), "Robin," "Cassandra," "The Albatross"

The Eras Tour Surprise Song Mash-Up: "Cowboy Like Me," "White Horse," "I Look in People's Windows," "Come Back...Be Here," "Daylight"

25 MINUTES

Taylor Swift: "Tim McGraw," "Teardrops on My Guitar," "Our Song," "Picture to Burn," "Should've Said No," "Cold as You," "Invisible"

Fearless: "Fearless," "You Belong with Me," "Love Story," "Forever & Always," "Breathe," "Untouchable"

Speak Now: "Long Live," "Timeless" (From the Vault), "The Story of Us," "Enchanted," "Sparks Fly"

Red: "Red," "State of Grace" (Acoustic Version), "Starlight," "Stay Stay Stay," "Run" (From the Vault), "We Are Never Ever Getting Back Together"

1989: "New Romantics," "Clean," "Out of the Woods," "Say Don't Go," "How You Get the Girl," "Style"

Reputation: "Ready for It?," "I Did Something Bad," "Delicate," "Call It What You Want," "Don't Blame Me," "Dress," "This Is Why We Can't Have Nice Things"

Lover: "I Forgot That You Existed," "Cruel Summer," "Paper Rings," "Cornelia Street," "Death by a Thousand Cuts," "The Archer," "Lover"

folklore: "The 1," "Invisible String," "August," "My Tears Ricochet," "Betty," "Illicit Affairs" *evermore:* "Champagne Problems," "No Body, No Crime" (ft. HAIM), "Coney Island" (ft. The National), "Cowboy Like Me," "evermore" (ft. Bon Iver), "Long Story Short"

Midnights: "Midnight Rain," "Maroon," "Anti-Hero," "Labyrinth," "The Great War," "High Infidelity," "Mastermind"

The Tortured Poets Department: "Fresh Out the Slammer," "loml," "The Alchemy," "So High School," "But Daddy I Love Him," "Cassandra"

The Eras Tour Surprise Song Mash-Up: "New Year's Day," "The Manuscript," "Long Live," "I Almost Do," "Out of the Woods," "Daylight"

30 MINUTES

Taylor Swift: "Mary's Song (Oh My My My)," "Teardrops on My Guitar," "Our Song," "Picture to Burn," "Should've Said No," "A Place in This World," "Cold as You," "Tim McGraw"

Fearless: "Fearless," "That's When" (From the Vault), "Fifteen," "Forever & Always" (Piano Version), "The Way I Loved You," "Change," "The Best Day"

Speak Now: "Back to December," "Electric Touch" (From the Vault), "Mean," "Dear John," "Haunted," "Last Kiss"

Red: "All Too Well" (10-Minute Version), "Treacherous," "Come Back . . . Be Here," "Everything Has Changed," "Sad Beautiful Tragic," "We Are Never Ever Getting Back Together"

1989: "Welcome to New York," "I Wish You Would," "Blank Space," "This Love," "Now That We Don't Talk," "Clean," "Suburban Legends," "You Are in Love"

Reputation: "Gorgeous," "King of My Heart," "Look What You Made Me Do," "This Is Why We Can't Have Nice Things," "Getaway Car," "New Year's Day," "Don't Blame Me," "Delicate"

Lover: "Miss Americana & the Heartbreak Prince," "Cruel Summer," "I Forgot That You Existed," "Lover," "Afterglow," "Paper Rings," "I Think He Knows," "It's Nice to Have a Friend," "The Archer" *folklore:* "Cardigan," "The Last Great American Dynasty," "Invisible String," "August," "Peace," "Epiphany," "Betty"

evermore: "Willow," "Champagne Problems," "Ivy," "Happiness," "Dorothea," "Coney Island" (ft. The National), "Cowboy Like Me"

Midnights: "Snow on the Beach," "Vigilante Shit," "Bejeweled," "Sweet Nothing," "Paris," "Lavender Haze," "Dear Reader," "You're on Your Own, Kid," "Maroon"

The Tortured Poets Department: "Fortnight" (ft. Post Malone), "My Boy Only Breaks His Favorite Toys," "Clara Bow," "Imgonnagetyouback," "How Did It End?," "I Hate It Here," "The Prophecy," "The Bolter"

The Eras Tour Surprise Song Mash-Up: "This Love," "Mine," "Everything Has Changed," "I Wish You Would," "You're Not Sorry," "Forever & Always," "Last Kiss"

40 MINUTES

Taylor Swift: "Tim McGraw," "Picture to Burn," "Teardrops on My Guitar," "A Place in This World," "Cold as You," "The Outside," "Tied Together with a Smile," "Stay Beautiful," "Should've Said No," "Mary's Song (Oh My My My)," "Our Song"

Fearless: "Fearless," "Mr. Perfectly Fine" (From the Vault), "The Best Day," "Untouchable," "White Horse," "Forever & Always," "Bye Bye Baby" (From the Vault), "You Belong with Me," "Don't You" (From the Vault), "That's When" (ft. Keith Urban) (From the Vault)

Speak Now: "Long Live," "Enchanted," "Mine," "Castles Crumbling" (From the Vault), "Sparks Fly," "Ours," "Better Than Revenge," "The Story of Us," "Mean"

Red: "Begin Again," "Holy Ground," "The Very First Night" (From the Vault), "Sad Beautiful Tragic," "Babe," "Red," "Message in a Bottle" (From the Vault), "22," "The Last Time," "State of Grace"

1989: "Style," "Slut!," "All You Had to Do Was Stay," "You Are in Love," "How You Get the Girl," "New Romantics," "Out of the Woods," "Clean," "Is It Over Now?," "Suburban Legends," "Now That We Don't Talk"

Reputation: ". . . Ready for It?," "I Did Something Bad," "Delicate," "Call It What You Want," "King of My Heart," "Look What You Made Me Do," "Getaway Car," "Don't Blame Me," "Dress," "Gorgeous," "So It Goes"

Lover: "I Think He Knows," "Cornelia Street," "The Archer," "Death by a Thousand Cuts," "Miss Americana & the Heartbreak Prince," "London Boy," "You Need to Calm Down," "Afterglow," "Daylight," "Lover," "False God"

folklore: "Exile" (ft. Bon Iver), "Seven," "My Tears Ricochet," "Illicit Affairs," "August," "Cardigan," "Invisible String," "Betty," "The Last Great American Dynasty," "The 1"

evermore: "Gold Rush," "Champagne Problems," "evermore" (ft. Bon Iver), "No Body, No Crime" (ft. HAIM), "Happiness," "Ivy," "Dorothea," "Coney Island" (ft. The National), "Willow," "Long Story Short"

Midnights: "Lavender Haze," "Maroon," "Anti-Hero," "Snow on the Beach," "You're on Your Own, Kid," "Would've, Could've, Should've," "Bejeweled," "Karma," "Labyrinth," "Paris," "Dear Reader"

The Tortured Poets Department: "Who's Afraid of Little Old Me?," "But Daddy I Love Him," "The Tortured Poets Department," "Guilty as Sin?," "The Smallest Man Who Ever Lived," "Fresh Out the Slammer," "I Can Fix Him (No Really I Can)," "Florida!!!" (ft. Florence and the Machine), "I Can Do It with a Broken Heart," "The Albatross"

The Eras Tour Surprise Song Mash-Up: "Speak Now," "Better Man," "Forever Winter," "Sad Beautiful Tragic," "New Romantics," "The Best Day," "Ours," "So High School," "King of My Heart," "The Archer"

50 MINUTES

Taylor Swift: Listen to the entire album start to finish, minus "Teardrops on My Guitar" (Pop Version).

Fearless: "Fearless," "Love Story," "Fifteen," "You Belong with Me," "Breathe," "Change," "Mr. Perfectly Fine" (From the Vault), "That's When" (From the Vault), "Forever & Always," "Untouchable," "The Best Day," "Don't You" (From the Vault)

Speak Now: "Dear John," "Timeless" (From the Vault), "Back to December," "Electric Touch" (From the Vault), "Enchanted," "Haunted," "When Emma Falls in Love" (From the Vault), "Long Live," "The Story of Us," "Sparks Fly"

Red: "All Too Well" (10-Minute Version), "I Knew You Were Trouble," "Forever Winter" (From the Vault), "Run" (From the Vault), "22," "Holy Ground," "Message in a Bottle" (From the Vault), "Starlight," "I Almost Do," "Treacherous," "State of Grace"

1989: "Welcome to New York," "Blank Space," "Shake It Off," "Out of the Woods," "Say Don't Go," "Clean," "I Know Places," "Suburban Legends," "You Are in Love," "Slut!," "Style," "All You Had to Do Was Stay," "Now That We Don't Talk" (From the Vault)

Reputation: "End Game" (ft. Ed Sheeran & Future), "Gorgeous," "I Did Something Bad," "Look What You Made Me Do," "Delicate," "Don't Blame Me," "This Is Why We Can't Have Nice Things," "King of My Heart," "Getaway Car," "New Year's Day," "Call It What You Want," "Dress," "So It Goes…"

Lover: "I Forgot That You Existed," "Cruel Summer," "The Archer," "Paper Rings," "Death by a Thousand Cuts," "Cornelia Street," "You Need to Calm Down," "London Boy," "Miss Americana & the Heartbreak Prince," "Lover," "Afterglow," "Daylight," "The Man," "It's Nice to Have a Friend"

folklore: "The 1," "Mirrorball," "Peace," "Hoax," "August," "My Tears Ricochet," "Illicit Affairs," "Cardigan," "Exile" (ft. Bon Iver), "Invisible String," "This Is Me Trying," "Epiphany," "Seven"

evermore: "Willow," "Champagne Problems," "Gold Rush," "Happiness," "Ivy," "No Body, No Crime" (ft. HAIM), "Dorothea," "Coney Island" (ft. The National), "Cowboy Like Me," "evermore" (ft. Bon Iver), "Marjorie," "Long Story Short"

Midnights: "Lavender Haze," "Anti-Hero," "Maroon," "The Great War," "Sweet Nothing," "Paris," "Snow on the Beach," "Vigilante Shit," "Bejeweled," "Mastermind," "High Infidelity," "Labyrinth," "You're on Your Own, Kid," "Midnight Rain," "Glitch"

The Tortured Poets Department: "Fortnight" (ft. Post Malone), "Down Bad," "I Can Do It with a Broken Heart," "Clara Bow," "The Black Dog," "Imgonnagetyouback," "The Albatross," "How Did It End?," "So High School," "I Hate It Here," "The Prophecy," "Cassandra," "Robin"

The Eras Tour Surprise Song Mash-Up: "Cassandra," "Mad Woman," "I Did Something Bad," "Out of the Woods," "Mr. Perfectly Fine," "Never Grow Up," "Timeless," "Ivy," "This Is Why We Can't Have Nice Things," "Starlight," "Message in a Bottle," "You Are in Love"

60 MINUTES

Taylor Swift: Listen to the entire album start to finish, plus "Picture to Burn" and "Tim McGraw."

Fearless: "Fearless," "Fifteen," "White Horse," "You Belong with Me," "Change," "Forever & Always" (Piano Version), "You All Over Me" (From the Vault), "Mr. Perfectly Fine" (From the Vault), "The Way I Loved You," "Love Story," "Bye Bye Baby" (From the Vault), "Untouchable," "Hey Stephen," "Breathe" (ft. Colbie Caillet)

Speak Now: "Mine," "Sparks Fly," "Dear John," "Enchanted," "Castles Crumbling" (From the Vault), "Back to December," "Electric Touch" (From the Vault), "The Story of Us," "Long Live," "Haunted," "Better Than Revenge"

Red: "State of Grace," "All Too Well" (10-Minute Version), "Red," "Sad Beautiful Tragic," "Message in a Bottle" (From the Vault), "Begin Again," "Holy Ground,"

"We Are Never Ever Getting Back Together," "Treacherous," "22," "Babe" (From the Vault), "Forever Winter," "The Very First Night" (From the Vault), "Stay Stay Stay"

1989: "Welcome to New York," "Out of the Woods," "I Wish You Would," "Blank Space," "Style," "How You Get the Girl," "Suburban Legends," "Say Don't Go," "Clean," "You Are in Love," "Now That We Don't Talk," "New Romantics," "Shake It Off," "All You Had to Do Was Stay," "This Love," "Is It Over Now?" (From the Vault)

Reputation: Listen to the entire album start to finish, plus "End Game" (ft. Ed Sheeran & Future).

Lover: Listen to the entire album start to finish.

folklore: "Cardigan," "The 1," "Exile (ft. Bon Iver), "Seven," "Illicit Affairs," "August," "Mirrorball," "My Tears Ricochet," "Betty," "Peace," "The Last Great American Dynasty," "Invisible String," "Epiphany," "This Is Me Trying," "Mad Woman"

evermore: Listen to the entire album start to finish.

Midnights: "Lavender Haze," "Anti-Hero," "Maroon," "The Great War," "Sweet Nothing," "Paris," "Snow on the Beach," "Vigilante Shit," "Bejeweled," "Mastermind," "High Infidelity," "Labyrinth," "You're on Your Own, Kid," "Midnight Rain," "Dear Reader," "Karma," "Would've, Could've, Should've"

The Tortured Poets Department: "The Tortured Poets Department," "My Boy Only Breaks His Favorite Toys," "Down Bad," "But Daddy I Love Him," "Fresh Out the Slammer," "Who's Afraid of Little Old Me?," "I Can Fix Him (No Really I Can)," "The Black Dog," "Chloe or Sam or Sophia or Marcus," "So High School," "I Hate It Here," "thanK you aIMee," "I Look in People's Windows," "Peter," "The Albatross," "The Smallest Man Who Ever Lived"

The Eras Tour Surprise Song Mash-Up: "Better than Revenge," "False God," "Cowboy Like Me," "Cold as You," "Sparks Fly," "Sweeter Than Fiction," "Teardrops on My Guitar," "Hits Different," "Maroon," "You're on Your Own, Kid," "A Place in This World," "New Romantics," "I Forgot That You Existed," "Long Live," "New Year's Day," "The Manuscript"

I'd Do It Over and Over Again

There are some staple recipes that you'll want to make over and over again, including the piecrust used for Rose Garden Apple Pie (page 139) and Cherry Pie with Crystal Skies (page 126) and the versatile Miss Americana Buttercream Frosting (page 26) that can be used on cakes and cupcakes.

This section includes some of these recipes that you'll want to come back to time and time again.

Glazes & Frostings

The Delicate Glaze

Makes 2 cups

- 2 cups confectioners' sugar, sifted
- 2 to 4 tablespoons whole milk
- 1 tablespoon fresh lemon juice
- 1 teaspoon pure vanilla extract

1 Combine the sugar with 2 tablespoons of the milk, the lemon juice, and vanilla in a large bowl.

2 Whisk until a smooth glaze forms. If the mixture is too thick, add the remaining 2 tablespoons milk, a tablespoon at a time, until your desired consistency is reached.

Miss Americana Buttercream Frosting

Makes 5 cups

3 sticks unsalted butter, room temperature

4½ cups confectioners' sugar, sifted

½ teaspoon salt

1 tablespoon pure vanilla extract

4 to 5 tablespoons whole milk or heavy cream

1 Place the butter in the bowl of a stand mixer fitted with the whisk attachment and beat on high speed until light and whipped, about 5 minutes.

2 Reduce the mixer speed to low, then beat in the confectioners' sugar, ½ cup at a time, mixing well with each addition and scraping down the sides of the bowl as needed, until the buttercream is light and fluffy, 3 to 5 minutes.

3 Add the salt and vanilla, beating until incorporated.

4 Slowly add in the milk, beating for an additional minute until whipped and well combined.

Doughs

Pie, Pie, Baby Dough

Makes 2 disks of dough for one 9-inch pie

2½ cups all-purpose flour, sifted
2 teaspoons sugar
1 teaspoon salt
2 sticks cold unsalted butter, cubed
½ cup ice water, plus more as needed
1 tablespoon white vinegar or vodka

1 Combine the flour, sugar, and salt in the bowl of a food processor. Add the cubed butter and pulse until the mixture resembles pea-size crumbs. (Alternatively, whisk together the dry ingredients in a large bowl, then cut in the butter with a pastry cutter.) Transfer the dough to a large bowl.

2 Combine the ice water and vinegar in a small bowl. If you're using a food processor, slowly stream the liquid in and pulse to incorporate. If you used a pastry cutter, you pour in the water and use your hands to mix it in until the dough just comes together. You want it to feel moist and hydrated but not wet.

3 Shape the pie dough into a ball and cut the ball in half. Flatten each half into a disk, then wrap the disks individually in plastic wrap. Refrigerate for at least 2 hours before rolling and baking.

The Best Tart Dough

Makes one 10-inch tart shell

1½ sticks butter, room temperature

½ cup sugar

½ teaspoon pure vanilla extract

1¾ cups all-purpose flour, sifted

1 teaspoon salt

1 Place the butter and sugar in the bowl of a stand mixer fitted with the paddle attachment and cream together on medium speed until light and fluffy, about 4 minutes.

2 Reduce the mixer speed to low. Add the vanilla, flour, and salt and mix, scraping down the sides of the bowl as needed, until incorporated, 3 to 5 minutes.

3 Break the dough into pieces and use your fingers to press it into a 10-inch tart pan with a removable bottom. Press the dough evenly along the bottom and sides of the tart pan. Refrigerate the tart shell for 30 minutes before baking.

Choux Dough

Makes enough for 18 crullers, 18 to 24 churros, or 16 eclairs

½ cup whole milk

6 tablespoons unsalted butter

1 tablespoon sugar

½ teaspoon salt

¾ cup all-purpose flour, sifted

¼ cup bread flour, sifted

3 to 4 large eggs

1. In a medium saucepan, combine the milk, butter, sugar, salt, and ½ cup water and bring to a boil. Turn off the heat and stir both flours into the pot until thoroughly incorporated (no dry spots should remain).

2. Turn the heat to low and cook for 2 minutes, until a film forms on the bottom of the pot.

3. Transfer the mixture to the bowl of a stand mixer fitted with the paddle attachment and beat on medium speed until the bowl feels cool to the touch and the steam has evaporated, about 5 to 7 minutes.

4. Add in 3 eggs, one at a time, and continue beating, scraping down the sides of the bowl as needed, until well combined. The dough should be thick, glossy, and hold a V shape when you remove the paddle. If it's too stiff, beat in the remaining egg.

Long Story Short:

Adding in too many eggs or whites can result in a dense pastry, so make sure you check as you go to ensure the delicate batter is just right.

Pastry Dough

Makes enough for 16 danishes, 12 bear claws, or 8 pains au chocolat

- 2 teaspoons instant yeast (double check to make sure your yeast hasn't expired!)
- ⅔ cup warm water
- ¼ cup sugar
- 2 cups all-purpose flour, plus more for the work surface
- 1 cup bread flour
- 2 large cold eggs
- 1 teaspoon kosher salt
- 3 sticks European butter (at least 82% fat), room temp (we recommend Kerrygold)

1 Place the yeast, warm water, and sugar in the bowl of a stand mixer fitted with the dough hook attachment and mix on low speed until frothy, 1 to 2 minutes.

2 Increase the mixer speed to medium-low. Add both flours, the eggs, and salt and continue mixing, scraping down the sides of the bowl as needed. The dough will first form a shaggy mass, but after 3 to 5 minutes, it will look smoother.

3 Remove the dough from the bowl and shape it into a disk. Wrap the disk in plastic wrap and place in the refrigerator to chill overnight. It will double in size.

4 The next day, place the butter on a 12 × 12-inch sheet of parchment paper and fold the parchment over the butter. Using a rolling pin, flatten the butter in its parchment package into a 6 × 6-inch square. Refrigerate for 30 minutes before use.

BREAKFAST AT MIDNIGHT

Sweet Treats Perfect for Breakfast . . . or *Midnights*

It feels like a perfect night . . . for pastries at midnight. This section includes much-loved breakfast pastries, like cinnamon rolls, biscotti, and, of course, pop(star) tarts! Whether you choose to eat them at 8 a.m. or midnight, it's always the right time.

A cruller's distinctive shape—twisted, then curled into a ring—is what makes it stand out from a typical doughnut. With crisp exteriors and a light, airy inside, these crullers will have you sneaking into the kitchen for seconds. The lavender glaze provides a delicate floral touch that balances out the sweetness of the dough.

Impress your friends by making these for your next brunch. One bite and they'll be cheering, "More!"

Cruller Summer with Lavender Glaze

Makes 10 to 12 crullers

1 recipe Choux Dough (page 29)
Vegetable oil, for frying

GLAZE
Nonstick cooking spray
2 cups confectioners' sugar, sifted
2 to 4 tablespoons whole milk
1 tablespoon fresh lemon juice
1 teaspoon pure vanilla extract
Edible lavender or edible glitter, for sprinkling

1. Grease a 13 × 8-inch sheet of parchment paper with cooking spray. Fill a pastry bag fitted with a star tip with the choux dough. Pipe crullers onto the prepared parchment paper in 3-inch circles. Refrigerate or freeze until ready to fry, at least 1 hour.

2. Line a baking sheet with paper towels and set aside.

3. Fill a Dutch oven with 3 inches of oil and heat to 375°F.

4. Working in batches, add a few crullers and fry until golden brown, 3 to 6 minutes per side. Be careful not to overcrowd the pan, or the oil temp may drop too quickly.

Recipe continues

5 Carefully remove each cruller from the hot oil with a slotted spoon and transfer to the prepared baking sheet. Repeat with the remaining crullers, bringing the oil back to 375°F before each new batch.

6 **While the crullers are cooling, make the glaze:** Whisk together the confectioners' sugar, 2 tablespoons of the milk, the lemon juice, and vanilla in a large bowl until the mixture becomes a smooth glaze. If needed, add the remaining 2 tablespoons of milk, a tablespoon at a time, until the desired consistency is reached.

7 When the crullers are cool to the touch, dip the tops in the prepared glaze. Quickly, before the glaze hardens, sprinkle with edible lavender and enjoy! These are best enjoyed within 24 hours.

When summer gives way to fall, these cereal bars are a satisfying sweet morning treat or an afternoon pick-me-up. And the best part? You don't have to be on your own, kid, with these treats, as they are perfect to share with the friends you've made along the way.

Pair with a glass of milk or a French press coffee.

You're on Your Own, Kid, Cereal Bars

Makes 12 to 16 bars

- ½ cup creamy nut butter of your choice
- ½ cup honey
- ½ teaspoon pure vanilla extract
- 3½ cups honey nut dry cereal

1 Line an 8 × 8-inch pan with parchment paper and set aside.

2 Combine the nut butter and honey in a medium saucepan over low heat and cook the mixture for 3 minutes, stirring occasionally. Remove from the heat and stir in the vanilla.

3 Add the dry cereal and stir until completely coated. Dump the mixture into the prepared pan. Press down firmly on the bars using a piece of parchment paper to prevent your hands from getting sticky.

4 Refrigerate the bars for 1 hour before serving. Slice into the desired sized bar and eat like a little kid again.

Pop-Star Tip:

This recipe features honey nut dry cereal as a subtle nod to Taylor's favorite breakfast cereal. If you want to give these cereal bars some extra sparkle, mix in your favorite color sprinkles before transferring to the pan. You'll transform these simple bars into dazzling showstoppers in seconds.

Is it a breakfast food? It is a special treat? Pop(Star)-Tarts are always trying to find their place in the culinary world.

There is one thing for certain: These filled pockets are a crowd favorite. After all, they can be packed with fun flavors like cinnamon sugar, berry jam, or chocolate marshmallow and topped with icing, confetti sprinkles, or both.

Taylor famously made her own "Victory Pop-Tarts" version and gifted them to the Kansas City Chiefs football team—a kind gesture that didn't go unnoticed. Bake a batch to share with your favorite sports team, or freeze them for a quick sweet morning treat before taking on the day. Either way, these Pop(Star)-Tarts will find a sweet place in your heart.

Long Story Short:

If you are short on time, buy premade pie dough and let it come to room temperature. Then all you need to do is cut the dough into rectangles, fill, bake, ice, and bejewel, and you'll be all about these Pop(Star)-Tarts for a long, long time!

Victory Pop(Star)-Tarts

Makes 3 to 4 Pop(Star)-Tarts

DOUGH

- 3¾ cups all-purpose flour, plus more for rolling
- ½ cup granulated sugar
- 2¼ tablespoons salt
- 2 pounds cold unsalted butter, cubed
- 1⅔ cups ice water
- 2 teaspoons apple cider vinegar
- 1 large egg

FILLING SUGGESTIONS

- Assorted jams
- Cinnamon sugar
- Dark chocolate chips and marshmallow fluff

ICING

- 1 cup confectioners' sugar
- 2 to 3 tablespoons whole milk
- ½ teaspoon vanilla
- Sprinkles, for topping

1 Make the dough: Combine the flour, granulated sugar, and salt in the bowl of a stand mixer fitted with the paddle attachment. Add the butter and mix on low speed until

Recipe continues

the mixture resembles pea-size crumbs. (Alternatively, whisk together the dry ingredients in a large bowl, then cut in the butter with a pastry cutter.)

2 Combine the water and vinegar in a small bowl, then slowly stream the liquid into the flour mixture, mixing and scraping down the sides of the bowl as needed until the flour is fully hydrated and the dough comes together. You want the dough to feel moist and hydrated but not wet.

3 Flatten the dough into a disk and wrap it in plastic. Refrigerate for at least 1 hour before rolling out.

4 Roll out the dough between two pieces of parchment paper to ¼-inch thickness. Using a pizza cutter, cut out six to eight 3 × 4-inch rectangles.

5 Preheat the oven to 400°F. Line a baking sheet with parchment paper and set aside.

6 Meanwhile, beat the egg in a small bowl and set aside. This will be your egg wash.

7 Lay out the sheets of dough evenly on the prepared baking sheet. Spread 1½ tablespoons of your desired filling on half the rectangle sheets. Brush the edges of the dough with the egg wash. Add a top rectangle of dough to each of the bottom rectangles. Gently pinch the sides together, then crimp the edges with a fork. Use the fork to poke holes in the top. Brush the entire top with egg wash.

8 Bake until golden brown, 12 to 14 minutes.

9 **Meanwhile, prepare the icing:** Mix together the confectioners' sugar, 2 tablespoons of the milk, and the vanilla. If needed, mix in the remaining 1 tablespoon milk to thin the icing. Set aside.

10 Remove the Pop(Star)-Tarts and let cool on a wire rack.

11 Once cool enough to handle, spread the tops with icing and bejewel with some of your favorite sprinkles.

Your Monday morning doesn't need to feel like you're stuck in an endless February. Make a batch of these cinnamon rolls on Sunday and enjoy a Monday morning breakfast treat that will make you ready to start another workweek. With an ooey-gooey cinnamon-sugar center and sweet cream cheese frosting, these definitely won't make it through a fortnight, but they will stay fresh for 3 to 5 days in an airtight container.

It's a 2 a.m. Surprise!

Just like *The Tortured Poets Department* was a surprise double album, this recipe also has a surprise double feature. While the classic cinnamon-sugar center is amazing on its own, you can up-level this treat by swapping it with a filling inspired by one of Taylor's favorite fall drinks: a pumpkin spice latte. Simply swap the filling in the recipe and surprise your friends with these incredible autumn flavors. Perfect for the plaid-shirt days of fall.

- 1½ teaspoons instant yeast
- ⅓ cup granulated sugar
- ¾ cup whole milk, room temperature
- 3¼ cups bread flour, plus more for the work surface
- 2 large eggs
- 4 tablespoons (½ stick) unsalted butter, softened
- 1½ teaspoons salt
- Nonstick cooking spray
- 2 tablespoons unsalted butter, melted
- Cinnamon Roll Sugar (recipe follows)
- Cream Cheese Frosting (recipe follows)

Fortnight Cinnamon Rolls

Makes about 12 rolls

1 Combine the instant yeast, sugar, and milk in the bowl of a stand mixer fitted with the dough hook. Add the bread flour, eggs, softened butter, and salt and mix on the lowest speed for 3 minutes. Increase the speed a little and mix for an additional

Recipe continues

8 minutes, scraping down the sides of the bowl as needed. (No stand mixer? You can knead by hand—it will just take some strength and a few more Taylor songs.)

2 Place the dough in a bowl and cover it with plastic wrap. Let sit for 30 minutes on the counter or in the refrigerator overnight. If refrigerating, let sit for 10 minutes at room temperature before using. Preheat the oven to 350°F. Grease a 13 × 9-inch baking pan with nonstick cooking spray and set aside.

3 Lightly flour your work surface and rolling pin, then turn out the dough. Roll out the dough into an 18 × 12-inch rectangle. Brush the dough with the melted butter, then sprinkle the cinnamon sugar evenly over the rectangle. Using clean hands, roll the dough into an 18-inch-long log.

4 Cut the log into 1½-inch slices, then arrange the log slices in the prepared baking pan. Bake until golden brown, 25 to 30 minutes.

5 Let cool completely, then top with the frosting.

Cinnamon Roll Sugar

Makes 1¼ cups

½ cup plus 2 tablespoons packed light brown sugar
½ cup plus 2 tablespoons granulated sugar
1½ tablespoons ground cinnamon
¾ teaspoon salt

Stir together all the ingredients in a small bowl.

Cream Cheese Frosting

Makes enough for 12 rolls

2 tablespoons unsalted butter, softened
3 ounces cream cheese, softened
1 cup confectioners' sugar
¼ teaspoon pure vanilla extract
¼ teaspoon salt

1 Place the softened butter and cream cheese in the bowl of a stand mixer fitted with the paddle attachment and mix on low to medium speed until smooth, 3 to 5 minutes. Add the confectioners' sugar and mix until no lumps remain, about 2 minutes.

2 Add the vanilla and salt and continue mixing, scraping down the sides of the bowl as needed for another minute to fully incorporate.

2 a.m. Surprise Filling

Starbucks Lovers' Pumpkin Spice

Makes about 1½ cups

½ cup plus 2 tablespoons packed light brown sugar
½ cup plus 2 tablespoons granulated sugar
½ cup pumpkin puree
1½ tablespoons pumpkin pie spice
¾ teaspoon salt

1   Place all the ingredients in a small bowl and stir well to combine.

2   Use this mixture in place of the cinnamon sugar in step three of the Fortnight Cinnamon Rolls recipe.

These biscotti are like driving a new Maserati down a dead-end street. They are fast to make, but then you have to come to a complete stop (to let them cool down before cutting and baking them again). They are infused with vanilla and anise, a classic flavor combo that pairs well with almost anything.

This recipe will become as easy as memorizing all the words to your old favorite songs. Add it to your playlist of recipes to serve at holiday brunches, or simply dunk in coffee while you're watching the news.

Drivin' a New Maserati Biscotti

Makes 38 biscotti

6 tablespoons unsalted butter
⅔ cup granulated sugar
½ teaspoon salt
1 teaspoon pure vanilla extract
¼ teaspoon anise extract (optional)
2 large eggs
2 cups all-purpose flour, plus more for the work surface
1½ teaspoons baking powder
1 large egg white
Raw sugar, for topping

1 Preheat the oven to 350°F. Line a large baking sheet with parchment paper and set aside.

2 In the bowl of a stand mixer fitted with the paddle attachment, beat the butter, granulated sugar, salt, vanilla, and anise extract, if using, until the mixture is smooth and creamy, 5 to 7 minutes.

3 Add the eggs and continue beating until well incorporated, 2 to 3 minutes. Slowly add the flour and baking powder. Beat until the mixture just comes together. The dough will be sticky.

4 Lightly flour your work surface and hands. Divide the dough in half. Working with one half at a time, shape the

Recipe continues

dough into a 9½ × 2-inch round log, about ¾ inch thick. Gently press down on the log to smooth its top and sides. Place the log on the prepared baking sheet and repeat with the other dough half.

5 Whisk the egg white in a small bowl, then brush it on top of each log. Sprinkle raw sugar on top.

6 Bake the logs for 25 minutes. Remove them from the oven and let cool for 5 minutes.

7 Reduce the oven temperature to 325°F.

8 Cut each log into ½-inch slices using a sharp chef's knife or serrated knife. Do your best to make sure you are cutting straight up and down to ensure even slices of biscotti.

9 Arrange the biscotti in an upright position on the baking sheet and return to the oven. Bake for another 25 to 30 minutes, until they feel very dry and are beginning to turn golden. It's okay if they're still a little moist in the very center—they will continue to dry out as they cool.

10 Transfer the biscotti to a wire rack to cool completely. Store leftover biscotti in an airtight container at room temperature for 2 to 3 weeks.

It's Nice to Have a Friend:

The biscotti will last up to 2 to 3 weeks in an airtight container, making them the perfect baked good to make in advance of a brunch or gathering. Package them in a pretty tin to gift friends, family, or colleagues for the holidays.

Look what you made me bake! This easy banana bread is nutritious enough to keep your mind alive but sweet enough to make you feel like you are feasting on a dessert. The bread derives its nutty flavor from an almond-meal base while garnering most of its sweetness from maple syrup and overripe bananas.

Pair with a mimosa for a weekend brunch and toast your real friends!

I Rose Up from the (Banana) Bread

Serves 6 to 8

- 4 very ripe medium bananas
- 3 large eggs
- ¼ cup pure maple syrup
- 4 tablespoons (½ stick) unsalted butter, melted
- ½ tablespoon pure vanilla extract
- 1 teaspoon ground cinnamon
- 1 teaspoon baking powder
- 1 teaspoon baking soda
- ¼ teaspoon salt
- 3 cups almond flour
- 2 mini chocolate chips

1 Preheat the oven to 350°F. Line a 9 × 5-inch loaf pan with parchment paper and set aside.

2 Mash 3 of the bananas with a fork in a large bowl. Whisk in the eggs, maple syrup, butter, vanilla, cinnamon, baking powder, baking soda, and salt until combined.

3 Slowly add the flour and stir with a spatula until fully combined.

4 Pour the batter into the prepared loaf pan. Create a decorative "snake" using the remaining banana: Slice the banana in half lengthwise. Cut out a diamond shape at the end of one of the halves to make a face. Arrange the banana halves on top of the batter in alternating directions.

Recipe continues

5   Bake until golden brown and a toothpick inserted into the center comes out clean, about 50 minutes.

6   Transfer the loaf pan to a wire cooling rack. After 10 minutes, remove the bread from the pan and let it cool completely. Press the chocolate chip "snake eyes" into the diamond face.

The chatter won't get old about these scones. The scone itself is so simple—the true stars of the show are the toppings. You can decorate your scones with various flavors and colors for any era or season of your life. Maybe you want to share the scones with those you love(r) the most? The Delicate Glaze is perfect for any lovely occasion. Maybe you want to bring a peace offering to get rid of any bad blood? Then the chocolate chip crumble is the way to go! With several unique toppings, there is a flavor for everyone at your table.

Long Story Short:

Don't let your Palace of Scones crumble overnight. Store scones in an airtight container, and they'll be good for an extra day or two!

Palace of Scones

- 2 cups all-purpose flour, sifted, plus more for the work surface
- 3 tablespoons granulated sugar
- 1 tablespoon baking powder
- ½ teaspoon salt
- 5 tablespoons cold unsalted butter, cubed
- 1 cup heavy cream
- 1 teaspoon pure vanilla extract
- 1 lemon or citrus of choice, zested
- The Delicate Glaze (page 25)
- Toppings (page 55)

Makes 8 scones

1 Line a large baking sheet with parchment paper and set aside.

2 Whisk together the flour, sugar, baking powder, and salt in a large bowl.

Recipe continues

3 Cut the butter into the dry ingredients with your clean fingertips or a pastry cutter until the mixture resembles pea-size crumbs.

4 Make a well in the center of the dry ingredients, then add the heavy cream, vanilla, and zest. Stir to combine just until no dry spots remain.

5 Wrap the dough in plastic wrap and refrigerate for at least 30 minutes.

6 Lightly flour your work surface. Turn out the dough and pat it into an 8-inch round. Carefully cut the round into 8 equal triangle wedges using a sharp knife.

7 Place the scones, 2 inches apart on the prepared baking sheet. Refrigerate for 1 hour.

8 Preheat the oven to 400°F.

9 Brush the scones with heavy cream and sprinkle the tops with raw sugar. Bake the scones until golden brown, 20 to 22 minutes. Remove from the oven and transfer them to a wire rack to cool.

10 Let the scones cool completely, then glaze the tops. Decorate with toppings of your choice and share with friends!

Chart-Topping Ideas

Once you've glazed your scones, you can add a wide variety of toppings to make them unique and match the colors and aesthetics of any party. Here are some of our favorites, based on Eras:

- *Debut:* Matcha glaze
- *Fearless:* Edible gold glitter
- *Speak Now:* Grape jam
- *Red:* Crushed dried strawberries or raspberries
- *1989:* Colorful sprinkles
- *Reputation:* Chocolate chips
- *Lover:* Cotton candy
- *folklore:* Edible fresh or dried flowers
- *evermore:* Marmalade
- *Midnights:* Lavender glaze (see page 34) or culinary lavender buds
- *The Tortured Poets Department:* Coffee glaze

What's better than burnt toast? Well, pretty much anything, but we can guarantee this coffee cake most definitely is. A sweet base with a streusel-style crumble pairs perfectly with a hot drink on a crisp fall day. But whether you eat it at midnight or midday, there is never a wrong time for coffee cake.

One bite and you will be in love.

Coffee (Cake) at Midnight

Serves 12

TOPPING

- ½ cup packed light brown sugar
- ½ cup all-purpose flour
- 1 tablespoon ground cinnamon
- 2 teaspoons cocoa powder
- ⅛ teaspoon salt
- 4 tablespoons (½ stick) unsalted butter, softened

COFFEE CAKE

- 2 cups granulated sugar
- 1½ sticks unsalted butter
- 1 tablespoon plus 1 teaspoon baking powder
- ½ teaspoon salt
- 1 tablespoon pure vanilla extract
- 3 large eggs, room temperature
- 2⅔ cups all-purpose flour, sifted
- 1¾ cups plain whole-milk Greek yogurt

1 Make the topping: Place all the topping ingredients in the bowl of a stand mixer fitted with the paddle attachment and mix on low speed, scraping down the bowl as needed, until sandy and well combined, 3 to 5 minutes. Scrape into a large bowl and set aside. Clean the mixer bowl and paddle attachment for reuse in step 3.

2 Make the coffee cake: Position a rack in the middle of the oven and preheat to 350°F. Line an 11 × 9-inch baking pan with parchment paper and set aside.

3 Place the granulated sugar, butter, baking powder, salt, and vanilla in the clean bowl of the stand mixer fitted with the paddle attachment and cream together on low to medium speed until the mixture is soft, light, and fluffy, 3 to 5 minutes. Add the eggs, one at a time, allowing each to fully incorporate and scraping down the sides of the bowl as needed before adding the next.

4   Add a third of the flour, then a third of the yogurt, mixing before repeating with the remaining flour and yogurt.

5   Stop the mixer and gently fold the batter once or twice with a spatula to ensure the batter is well mixed. Scrape the batter into the prepared baking pan, then spread into an even layer.

6   Squeeze the prepared topping in your hands to create large clumps and evenly distribute them over the top of the batter.

7   Bake until the coffee cake is puffed and firm to the touch and a toothpick inserted into the center comes out clean, about 40 minutes. Cool the cake for at least 30 minutes in the pan before slicing.

KARMA IS A COOKIE

Cookies, Cookies, and More Cookies!

Sweet like honey, karma is a crumb
Sitting on my lap 'cause I ate it
Check the thermostat
Me and cookies vibe like that

Beloved classic cookies, like sugar cookies and chocolate chip, make an appearance in this chapter, but also represented are a gluten-free and vegan version of Taylor's famous chai cookie (so everyone on your squad can enjoy) and my shaker cookies, which can double as a noisemaker, so you can shake along to your favorite Taylor song.

Compared to a traditional cowboy cookie, my Cowboy (Cookies) Like Me have some tricks up their sleeves. Along with the usual components of oatmeal, pecans, and shredded coconut, this version includes both white and dark chocolate chips, along with salted pretzels, making these the ultimate sweet-and-salty treat. The best part? They are made with maple syrup rather than refined sugar—making them forever the sweetest con.

Cowboys and bandits alike would be happy to munch on these for a sweet midday pick-me-up.

It's Nice to Have a Friend:

Looking for a sweet gift for a party host? Present these cookies as a jarred ready-to-make mix! Simply layer the dry ingredients in a 1-quart mason jar (no need to toast the pecans for this version). On an index card, list the wet ingredients to add to the dry mix, along with the mixing and baking instructions below. Use a ribbon or string to lasso the index card to the jar. This promises to be a dazzling and thoughtful hosting gift!

Cowboy (Cookies) Like Me

Makes 12 cookies

- 1 cup pecans, roughly chopped
- 2 sticks unsalted butter, softened
- 1½ cups pure maple syrup
- 2 large eggs
- 1 teaspoon pure vanilla extract
- 2 cups plus 6 tablespoons all-purpose flour
- 1 teaspoon baking powder
- 1 teaspoon baking soda
- ½ teaspoon salt
- 1 cup old-fashioned oats
- 1 cup pretzel pieces
- ½ cup coconut flakes, sweetened or unsweetened
- 1 cup white chocolate chips
- 1 cup dark chocolate chips

1 Toast the pecans in a dry skillet over medium heat until fragrant, 3 to 5 minutes. Set aside and let cool.

Recipe continues

2 Place the softened butter and maple syrup in the bowl of a stand mixer fitted with the paddle attachment and beat on low speed until light and fluffy, 3 to 5 minutes. Add the eggs and vanilla, beating well and scraping down the sides of the bowl as needed, until incorporated.

3 In a separate large bowl, whisk together the flour, baking powder, baking soda, and salt.

4 Gradually add the flour mixture to the butter mixture, beating on low speed until just combined. Gently fold in the oats, toasted pecans, pretzel pieces, and coconut flakes. Add the white and dark chocolate chips, mixing by hand until everything is incorporated. Do not overmix.

5 Refrigerate the dough for at least 1 hour, or up to 24 hours.

6 Preheat the oven to 350°F. Line a baking sheet with parchment paper.

7 Scoop the chilled dough into 1-inch balls and place 2 inches apart on the prepared baking sheet. Bake until golden, 12 to 14 minutes. Let the cookies cool on the baking sheet for a few minutes before transferring them to a wire rack to cool completely.

'Cause when you have only 15 minutes and somebody tells you they want cookies, they can believe you when you say you can make them. These no-bake cookies are perfect when you're short on time but are still determined to whip up a sweet treat (and they can be made vegan!). Pulled together with just a few simple ingredients, you'll be serving these before you finish listening to a few of your favorite songs.

After all, time can heal most things—and these cookies can definitely heal your sweet tooth.

15-Minute No-Bake Cookies

Makes 24 cookies

- 1 stick unsalted butter, or ½ cup coconut oil, if vegan, plus more for greasing
- ½ cup whole milk, or ½ cup almond milk, if vegan
- 2 to 3 tablespoons unsweetened cocoa powder
- 1 cup sugar
- 1 cup creamy almond butter
- 1 teaspoon pure vanilla extract
- ¼ teaspoon almond extract
- ¼ teaspoon salt
- ¼ cup chopped dairy-free bittersweet chocolate
- 3 cups quick-cooking oats
- Sliced almonds, for topping (optional)

1 Line a baking sheet with parchment paper, lightly grease with butter or coconut oil, and set aside.

2 Melt the butter or heat the coconut oil in a medium saucepan over medium heat, then add the milk, cocoa powder, and sugar. Increase the heat and bring to a rolling boil, stirring constantly for 1 minute.

3 Remove from the heat and stir in the almond butter, vanilla and almond extracts, salt, and chocolate. Add the oats and stir to thoroughly combine.

Recipe continues

4   Using a 2-tablespoon cookie scoop, quickly drop the batter onto the prepared baking sheet. Top with sliced almonds, if desired. Transfer to the refrigerator for 30 minutes, or to the freezer for 15 minutes, to cool and set before eating. Store covered in the refrigerator for up to 5 days.

Long Story Short:

Add sprinkles or edible glitter to give these cookies some shimmer.

When the hot cider is flowing and you are bundled in your coat and mittens, these cookies will make all your holiday cookie wishes come true. With a standard sugar cookie base, you can cut out these cookies in the shape of Christmas trees, sleighs, or any festive shape your heart desires.

Feeling the holiday spirit? Invite your squad over to decorate with royal frosting and sprinkles! Spread extra cheer by bundling up a few cookies in a festive tin tied with holly and ribbon, and give them to friends and neighbors.

Christmas Tree Farm Sugar Cookies

Makes 24 cookies

- 2 sticks unsalted butter, softened
- 1 cup sugar
- 1 large egg
- 2 teaspoons pure vanilla extract
- 1½ teaspoons baking powder
- ½ teaspoon salt
- 3 cups all-purpose flour, sifted, plus more for the work surface
- A variety of royal icing colors, for decorating
- Festive sprinkles, for decorating

1 Preheat the oven to 350°F. Line two baking sheets with parchment paper and set aside.

2 Place the butter and sugar in the bowl of a stand mixer fitted with the paddle attachment and cream together on medium speed until light and fluffy, about 2 minutes.

3 Add the egg, vanilla, baking powder, and salt and continue beating, scraping down the sides of the bowl as needed, until combined and smooth.

4 Reduce the mixer speed to low. Gradually add the flour, mixing until the dough just comes together.

5   Lightly flour the work surface. Divide the dough in half. Working with one half at a time, roll out the dough to ¼-inch thickness. Cut out desired shapes and place on the prepared baking sheets, leaving at least 1 inch of space between the cookies.

6   Bake until the cookies look set but are still pale, 10 to 12 minutes.

7   Cool on the baking sheet for 5 minutes, then transfer to a wire rack to cool completely before decorating with icing and sprinkles.

With bright yellow shimmering between the crinkles of sugar dust, these lemon cookies stand out in a crowd. They are light and refreshing, with a bold lemon flavor, making them a nice edition for any season. For a twist of fate, you can swap the lemon juice for Key lime juice, giving these cookies a tangier bite and an aurora borealis–green hue. Perfect for a Saturday movie night with friends.

Crinkling (Eye) Lemon Drops

Makes 24 lemon drops

4 tablespoons (½ stick) unsalted butter, softened

⅓ cup granulated sugar

1 tablespoon lemon zest (from about 2 lemons)

1 large egg

1 teaspoon pure vanilla extract

½ cup whole milk

2 cups all-purpose flour, sifted

1 tablespoon baking powder

⅛ teaspoon salt

LEMON GLAZE

1 cup confectioners' sugar, sifted

Zest of 1 lemon

2 tablespoons fresh lemon juice

1 Preheat the oven to 375°F. Line two baking sheets with parchment paper and set aside.

2 Place the butter, granulated sugar, and lemon zest in the bowl of a stand mixer fitted with the paddle attachment and cream together on medium speed until light and fluffy, 2 to 3 minutes.

3 Reduce the mixer speed to low. Add the egg and vanilla and continue beating, scraping down the sides of the bowl as needed, for another 2 to 3 minutes.

4 Continuing on low speed, slowly pour in the milk. At this point the batter will look very loose and liquidy. That is okay.

5 In a medium bowl, whisk together the flour, baking powder, and salt. Add the dry ingredients to the wet mixture and mix on low speed until just combined and no dry spots

remain, 2 to 3 minutes. With a spatula, gently fold the batter a few times to ensure the ingredients are well incorporated.

6   Using a 1-tablespoon cookie scoop, drop the cookies onto the prepared baking sheets, spacing them about 1 inch apart. Bake for 10 to 12 minutes, or until the cookies are golden brown. Transfer to a wire rack to cool completely.

7   **Make the glaze:** Whisk together the confectioners' sugar, lemon zest, and lemon juice until smooth. Drizzle the glaze over the cooled cookies.

With just a few pantry staples, these nutty, buttery, sweet cookies are commonly made during the winter-holiday season, but they can be enjoyed all year long (yes, even as a beach snack!).

Want to make them a bit weird, but still beautiful? Add edible googly eyes for a Halloween treat, roll in peppermint candy for a Christmas twist, or spin in any color sprinkles to match the colors of your favorite holiday . . . or sports team.

Snow(balls) on the Beach

Makes 24 cookies

- 1½ cups confectioners' sugar
- 1 cup pecans
- 1 cup all-purpose flour, sifted
- ½ teaspoon baking soda
- ¼ teaspoon salt
- 8 tablespoons (1 stick) unsalted butter, softened
- 3 tablespoons granulated sugar
- 1 teaspoon pure vanilla extract

1 Position a rack in the center of the oven and preheat to 325°F.

2 Place the confectioners' sugar in a large shallow bowl and set aside.

3 Spread out the pecans on a baking sheet and toast until golden, about 8 minutes. Let cool, then transfer the nuts to a food processor and pulse until finely chopped (or you can chop by hand on a cutting board with a chef's knife). Transfer the chopped nuts to a medium bowl and whisk in the flour, baking soda, and salt.

4 Place the butter, granulated sugar, and vanilla in the bowl of a stand mixer fitted with the paddle attachment, and cream together on low speed until creamy, 3 to 5 minutes.

5   Reduce the mixer speed to low. Add the nut mixture and continue beating, scraping down the sides of the bowl as needed, until combined.

6   Line a large baking sheet with parchment paper. Using clean hands, roll the dough into balls, about 2 tablespoons per cookie. Place the dough balls 1 inch apart on the prepared baking sheet and freeze for 10 minutes to firm up.

7   Bake until lightly golden on top, 20 to 25 minutes.

8   Allow the cookies to cool slightly on the baking sheet. When cool enough to handle, roll them, two at a time, in the confectioners' sugar. Return the cookies to the baking sheet and allow them to completely cool for 1 hour before rolling in the confectioners' sugar again.

9   Store the cookies between sheets of waxed paper in an airtight container at room temperature for up to 2 weeks.

Everyone thinks they know a thumbprint cookie, but they know nothing about this version. The shortbread-style cookie with a lovely heart-shaped raspberry-jam center not only looks great on display, but they also taste delicious. One bite and everything around you just stops. While these cookies can be made at any time of the year, they are the perfect treat to share with your friends or loved ones on Valentine's Day.

Squad Goals:

Not in a Valentine's Day mood? Host a Palentine's Day on February 13, bake these cookies with your best pals, and put on the 2010 movie *Valentine's Day,* featuring Taylor.

There Is an Indentation Thumbprint Cookie

Makes 36 cookies

- 2¼ cups all-purpose flour, sifted
- ½ teaspoon salt
- 2 sticks unsalted butter, softened
- 1 cup granulated sugar
- 3 tablespoons packed light brown sugar
- 1 large egg yolk
- 1½ teaspoons pure vanilla extract
- ⅔ cup thick raspberry or strawberry jam

1 Line two baking sheets with parchment paper and set aside.

2 Whisk together the flour and salt in a medium bowl. Set aside.

3 Place the butter, ½ cup of the granulated sugar, and the brown sugar in the bowl of a stand mixer fitted with the paddle attachment and cream together on low speed until

Recipe continues

light and fluffy, 3 to 5 minutes. Add the egg yolk and vanilla and continue beating, scraping down the sides of the bowl as needed, until well combined.

4 Reduce the mixer speed to low. Add the dry ingredients to the wet and mix until just combined.

5 Place the remaining ½ cup granulated sugar in a small bowl. Using clean hands, roll the dough into balls, about 2 teaspoons per cookie, then roll the dough balls in the sugar until well coated.

6 Place the dough balls, spaced 2 inches apart, on the prepared baking sheets. Using your two thumbs joined at the base, press a heart shape into the center of each ball. Place the baking sheets in the freezer for 30 minutes.

7 Preheat the oven to 350°F.

8 Fill a disposable pastry bag with the jam. Use scissors to snip a small corner off the bag. Carefully fill each indentation with about ½ teaspoon of jam. Don't overfill—less is best!

9 Bake the cookies until the edges are light golden brown, 10 to 12 minutes.

10 Let the cookies cool on the baking sheets, then enjoy!

Cookies that you can shake, shake, shake? Whoaaaaa! Oh! Oh! Use your favorite cookie cutters (hearts or stars optional). A clear candy hardens inside a hollowed-out cookie. After the cookie completely cools, add sprinkles and place another cookie on top, sealing the sides with icing. You not only have a very fun, edible cookie, but you have a bonus noisemaker. Shake them while dancing and singing along with your favorite song or while cheering on your favorite sports team.

Squad Goals:

This recipe is perfect to make with a group of friends, as you can create stations for every step. And at the end, you can all cheer along with what you created together!

Invisible Locket Shaker Cookies

Makes 12 cookies

2 sticks unsalted butter, softened

1 cup sugar

1 large egg

2 teaspoons pure vanilla extract

1½ teaspoons baking powder

½ teaspoon salt

3 cups all-purpose flour, sifted, plus more for the work surface

ASSEMBLY

1 cup clear isomalt crystals

A variety of royal icings

Sprinkles

1 Preheat the oven to 350°F. Line two baking sheets with parchment paper and set aside.

2 Place the butter and sugar in the bowl of a stand mixer fitted with the paddle attachment and cream together on medium speed until light and fluffy, about 2 minutes.

Recipe continues

3 Add the egg, vanilla, baking powder, and salt and continue beating, scraping down the sides of the bowl as needed, until combined and smooth.

4 Reduce the mixer speed to low. Gradually add the flour, mixing until the dough just comes together.

5 Lightly flour the work surface. Divide the dough in half. Working with one half at a time, roll out the dough to ¼-inch thickness. (Pop-Star Tip: If the dough is too soft, stick it in the freezer for a few minutes to firm it up again.)

6 With a cookie cutter of your choice (we used hearts, but you can use sunglasses, stars, moons, Saturn!), cut out as many shapes as you can. Transfer the cutouts to the prepared baking sheet, spacing about 1 inch apart.

7 Use a smaller square or heart-shaped cookie cutter to cut out the center of each larger cookie. Set aside the discarded dough. Cut each cookie in the same place so it will match up when "glued" together.

8 Transfer the baking sheet with the cookie cutouts to the freezer for 10 minutes to firm up. This will help prevent them from losing shape when baking.

9 Bake until the edges of the cookies are golden, 8 to 10 minutes. Start checking on your cookies at the 5-ish-minute mark since cutout size, freezer temperatures, and oven temperatures can vary.

10 Let the cookies cool completely. Set one-third of them aside on a wire rack and transfer the remaining cookies to the second prepared baking sheet.

11 Preheat the oven to 265°F.

12 **To assemble:** Bring the isomalt crystals to a boil in a small oven-safe saucepan or pot over medium heat. Once boiling (you'll see bubbles), remove from the heat completely. Allow the crystals to melt without stirring. Once the bubbles calm down, return the pan to the burner. Slowly add in 2 tablespoons water and stir. The isomalt will continue to bubble.

Recipe continues

13 Place the saucepan in the oven for 8 to 10 minutes. This helps remove the bubbles from the isomalt mixture.

14 Remove from the oven and carefully pour the isomalt into the centers of the cookies, spreading it to the edges. If the isomalt starts to thicken up while you are doing this step, place it back into the oven for a few minutes, allowing it to liquefy again.

15 Allow the isomalt in the cookies to completely cool, up to 15 minutes, before layering the shaker. You will need 3 cookies per shaker. (See Pop-Star Tip.)

16 Apply royal icing around the edges of one of the isomalt cookies, ensuring you stay away from the isomalt window. Stack with a non-isomalt cookie. This allows extra space for the shaking to occur!

17 Fill your cookie with sprinkles. Outline another isomalt cookie with royal icing and stack to seal.

18 Decorate the top of each cookie with royal icing and sprinkles.

19 Then shake, shake, shake and celebrate your creation before taking a big bite and watching the confetti sprinkles fall to the floor!

Pop-Star Tip:

If the clear isomalt is a little cloudy, put a little vegetable oil on a paper towel and carefully clean it, as you would with a dirty mirror or window. This will make it shiny and see-through for the sprinkles.

Note: Depending on the size of your cookie cutters, you can always make more or less by adjusting this recipe.

Why be every other black-and-white cookie when you can be the one with screaming color sprinkles? Taking the classic black-and-white cookie to the next level, we added colorful sprinkles that will surely make it stand out in a crowd. But don't worry, these cookies weren't built to fall apart. While they have a fluffy inside, their sturdy exterior keeps them intact.

This is one of those recipes that you'll want to repeat over and over again.

Black-and-White Cookies with Screaming Color Sprinkles

Makes 24 cookies

- 2 sticks unsalted butter, softened
- 1¾ cups granulated sugar
- 4 large eggs, room temperature
- 1½ cups whole milk
- ½ teaspoon pure vanilla extract
- ¼ teaspoon lemon extract
- 2½ cups cake flour, sifted
- 2½ cups all-purpose flour, sifted
- ½ teaspoon baking powder
- ½ teaspoon salt
- 4 cups confectioners' sugar
- 3 ounces bittersweet chocolate
- 1 teaspoon light corn syrup
- 1 to 2 tablespoons unsweetened cocoa
- Colorful sprinkles, for decorating

1 Preheat the oven to 375°F. Line two baking sheets with parchment paper and set aside.

2 Place the butter and sugar in the bowl of a stand mixer fitted with the paddle attachment and cream together on low speed until light and fluffy, 3 to 5 minutes. Add the eggs, one at a time, then the milk and both extracts, and mix, scraping down the sides of the bowl as needed, until smooth.

Recipe continues

3 Combine both flours, the baking powder, and salt in a medium bowl. Add the dry ingredients to the wet and mix on low speed until the dough just begins to form.

4 Using a 2-tablespoon cookie scoop, drop the dough onto the baking sheets, spacing 2 inches apart. Bake until the edges begin to brown, 18 to 20 minutes. Cool completely.

5 Bring 1 cup of water to a boil in a medium pot. Place the confectioners' sugar in a large heat-safe bowl. Gradually add enough boiling water to the sugar, stirring, to make a thick, spreadable frosting. Err on the side of caution because a too-thin frosting is hard to undo. Return the unused boiling water to the stovetop.

6 Spread the frosting on half of each cookie. Once all cookie halves have been frosted, place the bowl of the remaining frosting over the pot of hot water, creating a double boiler, and bring it back to a simmer. Stir in the bittersweet chocolate until melted, then the corn syrup and cocoa powder. Stir to thoroughly combine.

7 Spread the naked half of the cookies with the chocolate frosting. Before the frosting fully sets, top with the screaming color sprinkles. Let dry and enjoy!

Nonstick cooking spray

8 tablespoons (1 stick) vegan unsalted butter, such as Earth Balance, room temperature

½ cup vegetable oil

½ cup granulated sugar, plus more for topping

½ cup confectioners' sugar

¼ cup mashed banana

2 teaspoons pure vanilla extract

2 cups Cup4Cup gluten-free flour blend

½ teaspoon baking soda

¼ teaspoon salt

Tea from 1 chai tea bag (we recommend Tazo chai)

CHAI GLAZE

1 cup confectioners' sugar, sifted

1 tablespoon whole milk

½ teaspoon pure vanilla extract

Tea from 1 chai tea bag (we recommend Tazo chai), blitzed to a fine powder in a spice grinder

Ground cinnamon, for sprinkling

Ready to bake your first batch of cookies for the fall season? Taylor's classic chai cookies are a fall staple Swifties know and love. They first entered the Swiftie universe when Taylor posted the cookies on her Tumblr page. She made them for guests she invited to her 1989 Secret Sessions, a special event where she invited fans into her house and played her entire new record for them before it launched. Soon after, Taylor shared a handwritten recipe card for all to enjoy. While this cookie tastes like Christmas in September, it can be made and enjoyed the entire fall season. I've tweaked her recipe to make it both gluten-free and vegan, so no one feels left out during cookie time.

If you sprinkle too much cinnamon on one cookie, or thirteen, because the excitement of fall cannot be contained, it's okay. We aren't counting or taking names.

Chai Cookies à la Taylor

Makes 12 cookies

1 Preheat the oven to 350°F. Grease a baking sheet with cooking spray and set aside.

2 Place the butter and vegetable oil in the bowl of a stand mixer fitted with the paddle attachment and mix on low speed to combine.

Recipe continues

3 Add both sugars, the mashed banana, and the vanilla. Continue mixing until smooth, about 5 minutes. Stir in the flour, baking soda, salt, and tea until incorporated.

4 Cover the bowl with plastic wrap and transfer the dough to the refrigerator to chill for about 1 hour.

5 Using a 1-tablespoon cookie scoop, drop the dough onto the greased baking sheet, spacing about 1 inch apart. Press down evenly on each cookie and generously sprinkle the tops with sugar.

6 Bake until the edges are golden brown, 9 to 10 minutes. Let cool completely on the baking sheet before glazing.

7 **Make the chai glaze:** Combine the confectioners' sugar with 2 tablespoons of the milk, the vanilla, and chai powder.

8 Whisk until mixture is a smooth glaze. If it needs to be thinned, whisk in more of the remaining 2 tablespoons milk, a tablespoon at a time, until your desired consistency is reached. Spread the glaze over the tops of the cooled cookies, add a dusting of cinnamon, and enjoy!

These light pink macarons taste like rosé, not your roommate's cheap screw-top kind but the kind with a cork that you'd bust out for a big celebration.

While you can certainly enjoy these macarons as is, we recommend polishing them with specialty isomalt diamonds for an added bejeweled touch. You can find isomalt diamonds premade online, or you can purchase isomalts at a craft or baking store and melt them into diamond molds.

No diamonds? No problem. Sprinkle them with some edible glitter instead. Either way, when you walk into a room with these macarons, they'll definitely make the whole place shimmer.

So Scarlet, It Was Macaron

Makes 36 macarons

2 cups almond flour

2 cups confectioners' sugar

¼ teaspoon fine salt

7 large egg whites, room temperature, divided

1 cup granulated sugar

Pink food coloring paste, to color the macarons (optional)

FILLING

4 tablespoons (½ stick) unsalted butter, softened

1½ cups confectioners' sugar, sifted, plus more as needed

⅓ cup freeze-dried strawberry powder

2 to 4 tablespoons whole milk, as needed

OPTIONAL DECORATIONS

Edible glitter paint

Isomalt gemstones

1 Sift together the almond flour, confectioners' sugar, and salt in a large bowl. Whisk to combine.

2 Make a well in the center of the almond flour mixture and add 3 of the egg whites. Using a rubber spatula, fold and stir to make a paste. Set aside.

3 Place the granulated sugar in a small pot and add ⅔ cup water. Stir to combine. Wet your clean fingertips or a pastry

Recipe continues

brush and wash down any sugar crystals on the side of the pot.

4 Heat on medium-high heat without stirring until the mixture reaches 238°F on a candy thermometer.

5 While you are waiting for the syrup to reach temperature, place the remaining 4 egg whites in the bowl of a stand mixer fitted with the whisk attachment. Whisk on medium-high speed until they reach medium peaks, 5 to 7 minutes.

6 Once the sugar syrup has reached 238°F, bring the egg whites back together with a quick mix on medium speed, then slowly drizzle in the syrup in a thin, steady stream, continuing to mix until fully incorporated into the egg whites.

7 Increase the speed to medium-high and continue whisking, scraping down the sides of the bowl as needed, until the egg whites are inflated, smooth, shiny, flexible, and still a little warm, about 1 minute.

8 If using food coloring, squeeze a few drops to reach your desired color into the meringue and whisk for another 5 seconds or until completely incorporated.

9 Scoop a small amount of the meringue with a rubber spatula and fold it into the almond flour mixture to lighten it up. Fold in about half of the remaining meringue using broad strokes until only a few streaks are left. Fold the rest of the meringue into the batter until no streaks are left. The batter should slowly drip off the spatula like lava and slowly settle flat, not leaving any peaks.

10 Prepare a piping bag with a ⅓-inch round piping tip (Ateco #803) and pour some of the macaron batter into the bag. Pipe four small dots of batter directly onto each corner of a 17 × 12-inch baking sheet, then place a piece of parchment on top. This will prevent the paper from lifting up in the oven.

11 Hold the piping bag vertically about ½ inch above the parchment paper and gently squeeze to pipe a 1½-inch circle without moving the piping bag. Repeat,

Recipe continues

leaving 2 inches between each piped macaron, until all the batter is gone.

12. Gently tap the sheet on the counter to remove any air bubbles. Let sit for about 30 minutes until the surface of the macaron is dry to the touch.

13. Preheat the oven to 300°F.

14. Bake the macarons, rotating halfway through, until the shell is hard and the center is still soft, 15 to 20 minutes. Let cool completely on the baking sheet.

15. **Make the filling:** Place the butter in a large bowl and cream with a hand mixer on medium speed for about 1 minute. With the mixer off, add the confectioners' sugar and strawberry powder. Beat on low speed to incorporate. Increase the speed to medium and cream until very fluffy, 3 to 5 minutes.

16. Add milk, a tablespoon at a time, if the buttercream seems dry or stiff, or a little more confectioners' sugar if it seems too runny.

17. To assemble, prepare a piping bag with a ¼-inch round piping tip (Ateco #802) and fill the piping bag with the buttercream. Flip half of the macaron shells upside down and pipe a circle of buttercream onto each half. Place the other half of the macaron shells on top of the buttercream, pairing as best as you can similar-size disks for uniform macarons.

18. If desired, bejewel the tops with edible glitter or isomalt gemstones for an extra-special treat. Store covered in the refrigerator for up to 5 days, or in the freezer for up to 1 month.

Dear baker, if it feels like gingersnap season, then it is.

If you don't recognize these gingersnaps from the store-bought brands, then you did it right because these are better.

And while you can definitely enjoy these cookies alone while playing solitaire, we recommend sharing them at your next book club or board game gathering with friends.

Bend When You Can, Gingersnap When You Have To

- 2 cups all-purpose flour, sifted
- 1 tablespoon ground ginger
- 1 teaspoon ground cinnamon
- ¼ teaspoon ground cloves
- ½ teaspoon salt
- 1 teaspoon baking powder
- ½ teaspoon baking soda
- 1 cup vegetable oil
- ⅓ cup blackstrap molasses
- 1 cup packed light brown sugar
- ½ cup granulated sugar, plus more for rolling
- 1 large egg
- 1 teaspoon pure vanilla extract

Makes 16 cookies

1 Whisk together the flour, ginger, cinnamon, cloves, salt, baking powder, and baking soda in a medium bowl. Set aside.

2 Whisk together the oil, molasses, both sugars, the egg, and vanilla in a large bowl until smooth. Add dry ingredients to the wet and mix until just combined. Refrigerate the dough for 1 hour to firm up.

3 Preheat the oven to 350°F and line two baking sheets with parchment paper.

Recipe continues

4   Place some additional granulated sugar in a shallow bowl. With clean hands, roll 3 tablespoons of the cookie dough into a ball, roll in the sugar to coat, then place on one of the prepared baking sheets. Repeat with the remaining dough, spacing the cookies 2 inches apart. The dough will still be quite soft!

5   Bake until the edges are barely set and the tops are crinkled, 12 to 15 minutes. Let cool on the baking sheets for 10 to 15 minutes before serving.

The chocolate chip cookie is one of the most loved, adored, and greatest cookies of all time (kind of like a certain pop star we know and love)! There's just something about this cookie that feels like home—and this recipe's addition of buckwheat, a common grain used in many Pennsylvania baked goods, pays homage to Taylor's childhood hometown.

This chewy, nutty, chocolaty cookie (with a finished salty bite) is perfect for dunking in a cold glass of milk or for sippin' coffee with at midnight.

Squad Goals:

If you are making these for your squad and someone is gluten-free, you can simply swap the all-purpose flour with a no-gluten substitute, like Cup4Cup gluten-free flour blend. Buckwheat is a naturally gluten-free grain, so your friends will still get to enjoy the nutty richness this cookie brings—sans gluten.

Buckwheat Chocolate Chip Cookie (10-Minute Version)

Makes 24 cookies

- 8 tablespoons (1 stick) unsalted butter, softened
- ½ cup packed light brown sugar
- ⅓ cup granulated sugar
- 1 large egg
- 1 teaspoon pure vanilla extract
- 1 cup all-purpose flour
- ½ cup buckwheat flour
- ½ teaspoon baking soda
- ½ teaspoon salt
- 1½ cups dark chocolate chunks
- Flaky sea salt, such as Maldon, for topping

Recipe continues

1 Place the softened butter, brown sugar, and granulated sugar in the bowl of a stand mixer fitted with the paddle attachment and cream together on low speed until fluffy, about 3 minutes.

2 Add the egg and vanilla to the mixture and continue beating, scraping down the sides of the bowl as needed, until combined.

3 In a separate bowl, stir together both flours, the baking soda, and salt. Stir in the chocolate chunks. Gradually add the dry ingredients to the wet and mix on low speed until just combined.

4 Cover the bowl with plastic wrap and transfer the dough to the refrigerator for 30 minutes to firm up.

5 Preheat the oven to 350°F. Line a baking sheet with parchment paper.

6 Using a 1-tablespoon cookie scoop, drop the dough onto the prepared baking sheet, spacing 2 inches apart, and bake until the cookies are golden, 12 to 14 minutes.

7 Sprinkle some flaky salt on top of the cookies as they cool. Serve warm or at room temperature.

I BET YOU THINK ABOUT CAKE

Cakes, Cupcakes, and Bars

I bet you'll be thinking about *all* the cakes, cupcakes, brownies, and other cake-like treats in this section. While they don't fit into the upper-crust circles, they certainly do leave an impression. These treats will be a part of your wildest dreams, forevermore.

While this brownie recipe doesn't actually contain seven bars of chocolate, it is full of cocoa powder plus milk chocolate, white chocolate, and dark chocolate, making it perfect for any tortured chocolate lover who can't decide which kind to commit to. These brownies are the kind of flawless we wish every brownie could be.

Seven Bars of Chocolate Brownie

Makes 12 brownies

Nonstick cooking spray

2 sticks unsalted butter

¾ cup chopped dark chocolate

2 teaspoons pure vanilla extract

1 teaspoon espresso powder

½ teaspoon salt

1¾ cups granulated sugar

¼ cup packed light or dark brown sugar

4 large eggs, room temperature

1 cup all-purpose flour, sifted

½ cup Dutch-process cocoa powder, sifted

1 cup mixed milk chocolate, dark chocolate, and white chocolate chips (or go with just one kind, if you prefer)

1 Preheat the oven to 350°F. Grease a 13 × 9-inch baking pan with cooking spray and set aside. Line your pan with foil, leaving an overhang of 2 inches on the long sides, and grease the foil with cooking spray. This will help you easily remove the cooled brownies from the pan before slicing.

2 Bring a couple of inches of water to a simmer in a large pot and place a large heat-safe bowl on top of it to create a double boiler. Place the butter and chocolate in the bowl and stir until melted and mixed. (Alternatively, place the butter and chocolate in a large microwave-safe bowl and heat on high for 30-second intervals, checking and stirring after each interval, until melted.)

3 Transfer the bowl to the counter. Stir in the vanilla, espresso powder, and salt. Whisk in both sugars until smooth.

Recipe continues

4 Add the eggs, one at a time, whisking to blend after each addition, then continue to whisk until the batter is well combined, no more than 1 minute. This will help create the crackly, shiny top on the brownies.

5 Fold in the flour and cocoa powder until just combined.

6 Pour the batter into the prepared pan and sprinkle with the chocolate chips. Bake until the brownie mixture has puffed and is set and a tester inserted into the center comes out clean, 22 to 25 minutes.

7 Allow the brownies to completely cool in the pan, then use the foil overhang to lift the uncut brownies out of the pan. Use a sharp knife and cut into squares.

We're making these blondies with or without chocolate chips! While blondies are similar to a brownie in texture and shape, they use brown sugar instead of cocoa powder, giving them a blond color and a butterscotch flavor. This version includes chopped walnuts, but you can also add chocolate chips if you want to make them a little sweeter than fiction. However, we think these blondies are pretty perfect as is, just like our very own Blondie, aka Taylor.

While Blondie is a nickname Swifties have given Taylor as a nod to her blond hair, there are many others, including Tay Tay, T-Swizzle, Becky, T-Swift, Nils Sjöberg, Dr. Swift, Dead Tooth, Miss Americana, or simply just Tay.

Blondie(s)!

Makes 12 blondie(s)

Nonstick cooking spray

8 tablespoons (1 stick) unsalted butter

1 cup packed light brown sugar

¼ teaspoon kosher salt

1 large egg

1 teaspoon pure vanilla extract

1¼ cups all-purpose flour, sifted

½ teaspoon baking powder

1 cup white chocolate chips

¼ cup chopped nuts, toasted

¼ cup shredded sweetened coconut

¼ teaspoon flaky sea salt, such as Maldon (optional)

1 Preheat the oven to 350°F. Grease an 8 × 8-inch baking pan with cooking spray. Line your pan with foil, leaving an overhang of 2 inches on the long sides, and grease the foil with cooking spray. This will help you easily remove the cooled blondies from the pan before slicing.

2 Melt the butter in a small saucepan over low-medium heat, stirring occasionally, until the butter begins to foam and then brown. Remove from the heat once the butter turns golden brown and smells nutty. Pour the butter into a large bowl and let cool before using.

Recipe continues

3 Mix the brown sugar and salt into the cooled butter. Add the egg and vanilla and whisk until smooth and shiny.

4 Fold in the flour and baking powder with a flexible silicone spatula until just combined, then gently mix in the chocolate chips, nuts, and coconut.

5 Scrape the batter into the prepared pan and smooth it into an even layer. Sprinkle some flaky salt on top, if desired.

6 Bake until the edges are golden brown and a toothpick inserted into the center comes out clean, 20 to 25 minutes. Allow the blondies to completely cool in the pan, then use the foil overhang to lift the uncut blondies out of the pan. Use a sharp knife and cut into squares. Enjoy!

I Bet You Think About Cupcakes

Makes 13 cupcakes

Whether you're at a cool indie concert or at your house just watching TV, it's easy to dream about cupcakes. After all, a cupcake is basically a personal cake in a portable package. That's hard to forget.

This red velvet cupcake pays homage to the big cake featured in the "I Bet You Think About Me" music video. With Miss Americana Buttercream Frosting, you'll definitely want to dip in your finger and try before devouring the entire cupcake.

This recipe makes a baker's dozen, aka thirteen, which also happens to be Taylor's favorite number. She was born on December 13, 1989. Her first album went gold in thirteen weeks. Her first song that reached number one had a thirteen-second intro. She even used to write the number 13 on the back of her hand for shows during the Fearless tour. So it's no surprise that the number 13 has become synonymous with good luck for Taylor.

And lucky you, with the extra cupcake, you can snag one for yourself after sharing with your friends.

- 1¼ cups all-purpose flour
- 1 cup sugar
- ¼ cup unsweetened cocoa powder
- ½ teaspoon baking soda
- ¼ teaspoon salt
- 1 large egg, room temperature
- ½ cup vegetable oil
- ½ cup buttermilk, room temperature
- 1 tablespoon liquid or gel red food coloring
- 1 teaspoon white vinegar
- 1 teaspoon pure vanilla extract
- Miss Americana Buttercream Frosting (page 26)

Recipe continues

1 Set an oven rack in the center position and preheat the oven to 350°F. Place a cupcake liner in each well of a 12-cup muffin tin. Line just one well of a second muffin tin and set aside.

2 Whisk together the flour, sugar, cocoa powder, baking soda, and salt in a medium bowl.

3 Beat the egg in a large bowl. Whisk in the vegetable oil, buttermilk, food coloring, vinegar, and vanilla until smooth.

4 Gradually add the dry ingredients to the wet ingredients, mixing until just combined. Do not overmix.

5 Divide the batter evenly among the cupcake liners, filling each about two-thirds full.

6 Bake until lightly golden on top and a toothpick inserted into the center comes out clean, 18 to 20 minutes. Let the cupcakes cool in the tin for 5 minutes, then transfer them to a wire rack to cool completely.

7 Once the cupcakes are completely cool, apply the frosting with either a piping bag or a spatula.

These cupcakes have a vanilla buttermilk base with a classic vanilla buttercream frosting. Don't let the simplicity play you for a fool. The true star of the show is the decoration. While you can definitely sprinkle with your favorite Lover-era sprinkles, we suggest taking it a step further and garnishing with cotton candy, reminiscent of the blues and purple-pink skies. You'll feel like you are on cloud nine after one bite.

Pop-Star Tip:

If you want your cupcakes to look stage ready to bring to a Taylor-inspired par-tay, use cupcake liners that match the pastel Lover era.

Lover Cupcakes

Makes 12 cupcakes

Nonstick cooking spray
8 tablespoons (1 stick) unsalted butter, softened
¾ cup sugar
2 large eggs, room temperature
1 tablespoon pure vanilla extract
1¼ cups all-purpose flour, sifted
1¼ teaspoons baking powder
1 teaspoon salt
½ cup buttermilk, room temperature
Miss Americana Buttercream Frosting (page 26)
Cotton candy, for decorating

1 Set an oven rack in the center position and preheat the oven to 350°F. Line the wells of a 12-cup muffin tin with cupcake liners, spray with cooking spray, and set aside.

2 Place the softened butter and sugar in the bowl of a stand mixer fitted with the paddle attachment and cream together on medium-high speed until pale, light, and fluffy, about 5 minutes.

Recipe continues

3 Add the eggs, one at a time, and continue beating, allowing each egg to incorporate, and scraping down the sides of the bowl as needed, before adding the next. Mix in the vanilla.

4 Whisk together the flour, baking powder, and salt in a medium bowl.

5 Reduce the mixer speed to low. Add a third of the flour mixture, then ¼ cup of the buttermilk, scraping down the sides of the bowl as needed. Continue alternating between the flour and buttermilk, ending with the flour.

6 Divide the batter evenly among the cupcake liners, filling each about two-thirds full.

7 Bake until lightly golden on top and a toothpick inserted into the center comes out clean, 20 to 25 minutes. Let the cupcakes cool for 5 minutes in the tin, then transfer them to a wire rack to cool completely.

8 Once the cupcakes are completely cool, apply the frosting with either a piping bag or a spatula.

These sweet cake-like cookie sandwiches are considered a confectionary staple in Pennsylvania, Ms. Swift's home state. After one bite you'll be saying, "Yes, there are still beautiful things."

Pennsylvania Under Me Whoopie Pies

Makes 6 to 8 whoopie pies

Nonstick cooking spray

2¼ cups all-purpose flour, sifted

½ cup Dutch-process cocoa powder, sifted

1 teaspoon baking powder

½ teaspoon baking soda

½ teaspoon salt

1 cup packed light brown sugar

¼ cup vegetable oil

4 tablespoons (½ stick) unsalted butter, softened

1 large egg

1 teaspoon pure vanilla extract

¾ cup whole milk

¼ cup warm coffee

Whoopie Pie Filling (recipe follows)

1 Preheat the oven to 350°F. Line two baking sheets with parchment paper and grease with cooking spray.

2 Whisk together the flour, cocoa powder, baking powder, baking soda, and salt in a medium bowl.

3 Place the brown sugar, oil, and butter in the bowl of a stand mixer fitted with the paddle attachment and beat on low speed until light and fluffy, 2 to 3 minutes. Add the egg and vanilla and continue beating, scraping down the sides of the bowl as needed, until combined.

4 Add the dry ingredients and beat on medium-low speed until only a few dry streaks remain. Slowly stream in the milk, followed by the coffee, and beat until just combined.

5 Using a 3-tablespoon cookie scoop, drop the batter onto the prepared baking sheets, spacing 3 inches apart.

Recipe continues

6 Bake the pies until the edges are firm and the centers are just slightly soft, 10 to 12 minutes. Transfer to a wire rack to cool completely.

7 To assemble, arrange half of the cookies top side down. Fill a piping bag fitted with a round tip (Ateco #809) with the pie filling and pipe a circle of filling around the edges of the cookies. Continue piping the filling, working your way to the centers. Top with the remaining cookies to make a sandwich.

Whoopie Pie Filling

- 1 cup (2 sticks) unsalted butter, softened
- 1 cup creamy peanut butter
- 2 teaspoons pure vanilla extract
- 2½ cups confectioners' sugar, sifted

Place the butter and peanut butter in the bowl of a stand mixer fitted with the paddle attachment and beat on low speed until smooth, 3 to 5 minutes. Beat in the vanilla, then the confectioners' sugar, scraping down the sides of the bowl as needed, until well blended.

Another year older? Another reason to celebrate! This three-layer confetti sprinkle cake is perfect for a friend's birthday (or even to celebrate Taylor's birthday on December 13!). While the cake is great in and of itself, it also feels extra special for your own birthday.

And if you're a real mastermind, you can layer the cake with chocolate frosting instead of a standard vanilla, giving it a twist of fate.

Blank Cake for a Big Cake, Happy Birthday

Serves 8 to 10

Nonstick cooking spray

3 cups cake flour, sifted

2 teaspoons baking powder

½ teaspoon baking soda

1 teaspoon salt

12 tablespoons unsalted butter, softened

1½ cups sugar

4 large egg whites, whisked, room temperature

⅔ cup whole milk, room temperature

⅔ cup plain yogurt, room temperature

3 teaspoons pure vanilla extract

1 cup sprinkles

Miss Americana Buttercream Frosting (page 26) (one recipe will lightly frost the cake; double it for fully frosted)

1 Preheat the oven to 350°F. Line and grease three 8 × 3-inch round cake pans with cooking spray.

2 Whisk together the cake flour, baking powder, baking soda, and salt in a large bowl. Set aside.

3 Place the butter and sugar in the bowl of a stand mixer fitted with a paddle attachment and beat on high speed until light and fluffy, 3 to 5 minutes. Add the egg whites and continue beating, scraping down the sides of the bowl as needed, until combined.

Recipe continues

Long Story Short:

Time flies so if you find yourself running behind, a box (or two) of cake mix will work perfectly fine for the cake. Top with Miss Americana Buttercream Frosting, decorate, and enjoy!

4   Add the dry ingredients to the butter mixture and beat until just combined, 3 to 5 minutes.

5   Reduce the mixer speed to low. Slowly pour in the milk, followed by the yogurt and vanilla, and beat just until all the ingredients are combined. Do not overmix. Gently fold in the sprinkles.

6   Divide the batter among the prepared cake pans. Gently tap the pans on the counter to level the batter and release air bubbles. Bake until lightly golden and a toothpick inserted into the center of the cakes comes out clean, 25 to 35 minutes. Allow the cakes to cool completely in the pans.

7   To assemble, thinly slice off the very top of each layer horizontally with a serrated knife to help make them level for easier layering. Place the bottom layer on a cake stand and top with frosting, using a spatula to even out the frosting. Repeat with the second and third layers. For a full look, completely frost. For a naked cake, lightly frost the sides, keeping some of the cake peeking through. Either way, top the cake with sprinkles!

8   Store leftover cake in an airtight container at room temperature for up to 1 day or in the refrigerator for up to 5 days.

Welcome to New York! A classic New York cheesecake with a graham cracker crust and a crack-free smooth center, this is the cheesecake you've been waiting for. Plus, it's simple enough to make for even a culinary ingénue.

Everybody agrees that because this cheesecake is so rich, it pairs well with coffee or tea to balance it out, and, of course, it's the perfect midnight snack. Best served cold, like the first fall of snow.

Welcome to New York Cheesecake

Serves 8

CRUST

- 2 cups graham cracker crumbs
- ⅓ cup packed light brown sugar
- ¼ teaspoon salt
- 8 tablespoons (1 stick) unsalted butter, melted

FILLING

- 5 (8-ounce) blocks full-fat cream cheese, room temperature
- 1½ cups granulated sugar
- ½ teaspoon salt
- Zest of 1 lemon
- ⅓ cup full-fat sour cream
- 2 teaspoons fresh lemon juice
- 2 teaspoons pure vanilla extract
- 2 large egg yolks
- 6 large eggs

1 Make the crust: Set an oven rack in the lower third position and preheat the oven to 325°F. Grease the bottom and sides of a 9-inch springform pan. Set aside.

2 Stir together the graham cracker crumbs, brown sugar, and salt in a medium bowl.

3 Pour the melted butter over the mixture and stir with a fork until the crumbs are moistened. Press the mixture evenly into the bottom and up the sides of the prepared pan. Bake until the edges begin to lightly brown, 10 to 12 minutes. Set aside to cool.

Recipe continues

4 Make the cheesecake filling: Place the cream cheese, granulated sugar, salt, and lemon zest in the bowl of a stand mixer fitted with the paddle attachment and beat on medium speed until combined, 3 to 5 minutes.

5 Reduce the mixer speed to low. Add the sour cream, lemon juice, and vanilla and continue beating, scraping down the sides of the bowl as needed, until combined and smooth. It's important there are no lumps.

6 Add the egg yolks, beating well, then add the eggs, two at a time. Mix until just combined.

7 Pour the filling into the crust and place the springform pan on a baking sheet. Bake until mostly firm with a slight jiggle in the center, 2 hours and 15 minutes to 3 hours.

8 Cool the cheesecake in the pan to room temperature, at least 3 hours. Then cover tightly with plastic wrap and refrigerate overnight before serving. Store covered in the refrigerator for up to 5 days.

"Magical," "mad," "heavenly," and "sinful" are words used to describe this tiramisu, a traditional Italian dessert made with ladyfingers dipped in coffee, then layered between a creamy mascarpone whipped filling, and topped with a sprinkling of cocoa powder.

One look and guests will be saying that's a dessert that looks like their next mistake. But at this party, mistakes are forgiven, so grab a blank plate because there's a slice with your name on it.

New Money, Tiramisu(it), and Tie

Serves 12

- 1 cup brewed espresso or coffee, cooled
- 1 tablespoon pure vanilla extract
- 5 large cold egg yolks
- ½ cup sugar
- ½ teaspoon kosher salt
- 16 ounces mascarpone cheese
- 1¾ cups cold heavy cream
- 30 to 35 ladyfinger sponges
- ½ cup Dutch-process cocoa powder

1 Combine the espresso with the vanilla in a small bowl and set aside.

2 Beat the egg yolks and sugar in a stand mixer fitted with the whip attachment until pale and thick, about 5 minutes. Add the salt and mascarpone cheese and continue to whip until smooth. Slowly stream in the heavy cream and continue to whip until the filling is smooth and slightly thickened. Set aside.

3 Dunk each ladyfinger in the espresso mixture for just a second, then place in a 12 × 9-inch glass baking dish.

Recipe continues

4 Spread half of the whipped mascarpone over the first layer of ladyfingers in a smooth, even layer. Dust with cocoa powder.

5 Repeat the process and finish by dusting with more cocoa powder.

6 Cover tightly with plastic wrap and refrigerate for a few hours before serving. Store covered in the refrigerator for up to 5 days.

On a Six-Lane Texas Sheet Pan Cake

Serves 12 to 16

Did you know you can make a cake on a sheet pan? No specialty cake pan required. No, really, you can! Trust us, this cake is infused with so much butter, it can handle a dangerous (ungreased) pan.

Sheet cakes are thinner than traditional cakes, and this one is super moist and super chocolaty. The key to this cake is pouring the icing over it while it is still warm and serving immediately. The cake-to-icing ratio fits together like a perfect rhyme.

Make this dessert for your next potluck, a Super Bowl party, or while on vacation at your timeshare in Destin.

CAKE

- 2 sticks unsalted butter, softened
- 3 tablespoons Dutch-process cocoa powder, sifted
- 2 cups all-purpose flour, sifted
- 2 cups granulated sugar
- ½ teaspoon salt
- ½ cup buttermilk
- 2 large eggs
- 1 teaspoon baking soda
- 1 teaspoon pure vanilla extract

FROSTING

- 8 tablespoons (1 stick) unsalted butter, softened
- 6 tablespoons whole milk
- 3 tablespoons Dutch-process cocoa powder
- 1 teaspoon pure vanilla extract
- 2 cups confectioners' sugar, sifted
- 1 cup chopped pecans (optional)
- Flaky sea salt, such as Maldon, for topping (optional)

1 Make the cake: Preheat the oven to 350°F.

2 Heat the butter, cocoa powder, and 1 cup of water in a medium saucepan over medium heat. Stir until the butter melts, then remove from the heat and let cool.

3 Meanwhile, stir together the flour, sugar, and salt in a large bowl. Whisk in the butter mixture to combine.

Recipe continues

4 Whisk together the buttermilk, eggs, baking soda, and vanilla in a medium bowl, then whisk this mixture into the flour mixture until thoroughly combined.

5 Pour the batter into a quarter sheet pan. Bake until the center springs back when touched and a toothpick inserted into the center comes out clean, about 20 minutes. Allow the cake to cool on the sheet pan for 5 minutes before frosting.

6 **Make the frosting:** Combine the butter, milk, cocoa powder, and vanilla in a large saucepan over medium heat. Stir until the butter melts, then whisk in the confectioners' sugar until there are no lumps.

7 Spread the warm frosting over the slightly cool cake. Top with chopped pecans and flaky salt, if desired.

8 Allow the cake to cool completely before slicing with a sharp knife.

Taylor's debut single, "Tim McGraw," put her on the map as a country artist. The song hit the Top 40 Billboard chart in the summer of 2006. This cake cone is an ode to Taylor's country roots and debut summer release. These cupcakes are made with a store-bought cake mix, cake cones, frosting, melting candy, and decorative toppings.

Pop-Star Tip:

Want homemade cake cones instead? Replace the cake mix with Lover Cupcakes (page 104) and double the recipe to make 24 cones.

When You Think Tim McGraw Cake Cones

Makes 24 cones

24 flat-bottom cake cones

1 (15.25-ounce) box Funfetti cake mix

Pink melting candy

Frosting of choice

Sprinkles, gumdrops, or other bejeweled toppings, for decoration

1 Preheat the oven to 350°F. Place the cones in the wells of two 12-cup muffin tins.

2 Prepare the cake mix batter as directed on the package. Do not bake.

3 Fill the cones with about 3 tablespoons of batter, no more than two-thirds full. Do not overfill or the cupcakes will overflow.

Recipe continues

4 Bake until golden brown and a toothpick inserted into the center comes out clean, 18 to 22 minutes. Let cool completely.

5 Place the candy melts in a small microwave-safe bowl and heat on high temperature in 15- to 30-second intervals, checking and stirring after each interval, until melted.

6 Spoon the melted candy in shapes of dripping ice cream over the cake cone. Let cool completely.

7 Once cool, use a star pastry tip (Ateco #861) to pipe the frosting to resemble a soft-serve ice cream cone. Decorate with toppings of your choice.

PIE, PIE, BABY!

Pies, Tarts, and Other Doughy Treats

These pies and tarts feel like home somehow. They make you want to curl up with a good book and stay in bed the whole weekend. Cherry and pumpkin pies are just a couple of the classics you'll find in this section, but prepare to make new discoveries as well, such as a strawberry pretzel salad.

This might just be the last great American Pienasty.

The pie is both sweet and tart—pulling from the sweetness of condensed milk and the tartness of Key limes. While this pie is more popular in Florida!!!, it makes for a refreshing summertime treat anywhere you can get your hands on some Key limes.

Whether you decide to share this treat during a card game night with your pack of friends or as an "I'm sorry" gift to a neighbor you got in a feud with, you'll have a marvelous time baking, eating, sharing, or gifting!

Rebekah's Key Lime Pie

Serves 8

CRUST

- 1½ cups graham cracker crumbs
- ¼ cup sugar
- 6 tablespoons unsalted butter, melted

FILLING

- 2 (14-ounce) cans full-fat sweetened condensed milk
- 1 cup fresh Key lime juice (from 18 to 20 Key limes) or Nellie and Joe's Famous Key West Lime Juice
- 4 large egg yolks
- 1 teaspoon Key lime or lime zest, plus more for garnish

Whipped cream, for serving

Lime slices, for garnish

1 Preheat the oven to 350°F.

2 **Make the crust:** Combine the graham cracker crumbs and sugar together in a medium bowl, then stir in the melted butter. The mixture will be thick and sandy. Break up any large chunks.

3 Pour the mixture into an ungreased 9-inch pie dish. Using clean hands, pat the crumbs down into the bottom and up the sides of the pie dish to make a compact crust. Alternatively, you can use the flat bottom of a measuring cup to help you gently compress the crumbs together, but do not pack down too hard. The mixture should no longer be crumbly.

4 Bake about 10 minutes, then set aside to cool. Leave the oven on while you make the pie filling.

5 **Make the filling:** Whisk the sweetened condensed milk, lime juice, and egg yolks in a large bowl. Whisk in the lime zest. Pour the filling into the crust.

6 Bake the pie until mostly set with a very slight jiggle in the center, 18 to 20 minutes. Remove from the oven and let it cool completely. Once cool, cover and refrigerate for at least 1 hour before serving. Top with whipped cream and additional lime zest and/or lime slices to garnish. Store covered in the refrigerator for up to 5 days.

You got that classic cherry pie thing that we like! While cherry pies are made with sour cherries and topped with a checkerboard-style crust, this version keeps the sour cherries but tops with crystal skies—a cloud-shaped crust dusted with raw sugar cane and edible glitter paint. It's a showstopper worthy of any celebration. Grab a slice and get the rosé flowing with your chosen family and celebrate the good life.

Pop-Star Tip:

When it comes to baking, it's fun to experiment. Think of it like your tour rehearsals. You might not get everything right the first time, but all the practice helps you for your big show. Maybe you try using edible glitter paint for the first time and don't love how it turned out? That's okay! Even pop stars mess up every now and then. You can always shake it off and begin again.

Cherry Pie with Crystal Skies

Serves 8

1 recipe Pie, Pie, Baby Dough (page 27)

All-purpose flour, for the work surface

FILLING

4½ cups halved pitted fresh or thawed, frozen sour cherries

⅔ cup granulated sugar

1 teaspoon ground cinnamon

1 teaspoon ground ginger

Zest of 1 lemon

¼ cup cornstarch

1 tablespoon fresh lemon juice

1 teaspoon pure vanilla extract

1 tablespoon cold unsalted butter, cut into small cubes (use when assembling the pie)

ASSEMBLY

Heavy cream, for brushing

Raw sugar, for sprinkling

Edible glitter paint, for decorating (optional)

1 Lightly flour your work surface, rolling pin, and hands. Remove one of the prepared dough disks from the refrigerator and place on the work surface (keep the other refrigerated until ready to roll). Working quickly so the dough stays cold,

Recipe continues

roll out the dough, starting from the center of the disk, into a 12-inch round. Gently turn your dough with your hands between rolls to maintain an even thickness and shape. Fit the rolled-out dough into a 9-inch pie dish. Trim the edge with a small paring knife, leaving a 1-inch overhang.

2 Make the filling: Stir together the cherries, granulated sugar, cinnamon, ginger, and lemon zest in a large pot.

3 Whisk together the cornstarch, lemon juice, and vanilla in a small bowl until thoroughly combined. Stir into the cherry mixture. Place the pot over low heat and cook, stirring constantly, until the mixture begins to thicken. Once thickened, remove from the heat and let cool completely.

4 Preheat the oven to 400°F.

5 Pour the cooled filling into the prepared piecrust. Dot the small butter cubes on top of the filling.

6 To assemble: Remove the remaining disk of chilled pie dough from the refrigerator, roll it into a 12-inch round, then lay it on top of the filling. Trim the excess dough, leaving a 1-inch overhang. Roll out the excess dough and cut out cloud shapes. Gently press to seal with the bottom crust, then crimp the edges.

7 Lightly brush the top of the piecrust with the heavy cream, then place the clouds on top and brush them with cream. Sprinkle the top with raw sugar. Cut small vent holes into the top of the pie.

8 Place the pie dish on a large baking sheet and bake for 20 minutes. Reduce the oven temperature to 375°F and bake for an additional 30 to 40 minutes, until the crust is golden brown and the filling juices are bubbling and thick.

9 Let the pie cool completely on a wire rack.

10 Once completely cool, decorate the clouds with edible glitter to give them a little shimmer. Slice and serve! Store covered in the refrigerator for up to 5 days.

½ recipe Pie, Pie, Baby Dough (page 27)

All-purpose flour, for the work surface

FILLING

1 (15-ounce) can pumpkin puree (preferably Libby's)

3 large eggs

1¼ cups packed light brown sugar

1 tablespoon cornstarch

1 tablespoon ground cinnamon

¾ teaspoon ground ginger

⅛ teaspoon freshly grated nutmeg

¼ teaspoon ground cloves

½ teaspoon salt

⅛ teaspoon fresh ground black pepper

1 cup heavy cream

¼ cup whole milk

ASSEMBLY

1 egg, lightly beaten

2 tablespoons raw sugar

Oh, the sweet disposition of pumpkin pie—a fall delicacy available for about three months of the year—keeps us pining in anticipation of its yearly release.

Traditionally, pumpkin pie is made without a top crust, and you can certainly prepare it that way. However, if you have any leftover dough scraps, you can make a few autumn leaves for a festive touch.

Enjoy a warmed-up slice of pie with a dollop of whipped cream or grab a cold slice at 2 a.m. while you are dancing 'round the kitchen in the refrigerator light.

Autumn Leaves Falling Down Like Pieces of Pumpkin Pie

Serves 8

1 Lightly flour your work surface, rolling pin, and hands. Remove the prepared dough disk from the refrigerator and place on the work surface. Working quickly so the dough stays cold, roll out the dough, starting from the center of the disk, into a 12-inch round. Gently turn your dough with your hands between rolls to maintain an even thickness and shape. Fit the rolled-out dough into a 9-inch pie dish. Trim the excess dough, leaving a 1-inch overhang. Crimp the edges. Set aside the scraps in the refrigerator for later.

Recipe continues

2 Preheat the oven to 375°F. Line the pie shell with parchment paper and fill with pie weights (or dry, uncooked rice or beans). Par-bake for 10 minutes. Remove the crust from the oven and let cool enough so you can remove the weights and parchment paper. Leave the oven on.

3 Gently prick the bottom of the crust with a fork, then return it to the oven until lightly brown, another 8 minutes. Let cool.

4 **Make the filling:** Whisk together the pumpkin, eggs, and brown sugar in a large bowl. Whisk in the cornstarch, cinnamon, ginger, nutmeg, cloves, salt, pepper, heavy cream, and milk to thoroughly combine. Pour the filling into the cooled crust, no more than three-quarters full.

5 Bake the pie until mostly set with a very slight jiggle in the center, 55 to 60 minutes. After 25 minutes of baking, cover the crust with foil to prevent the edges from getting too brown. Check for doneness starting at 50 minutes and every 5 minutes thereafter until the pie is done.

6 Reduce oven heat to 350°F. While the pie is cooling, roll out the dough scraps and use a leaf cookie cutter to cut out the shapes. Lightly brush each leaf with the beaten egg and sprinkle with sugar. Bake until golden brown on the edges, 10 to 12 minutes. Let cool.

7 Allow the pie to cool completely, then refrigerate the pie until ready to serve. Just before slicing, arrange the pastry leaves on top of the pie to resemble fallen leaves. Store covered in the refrigerator for up to 5 days.

No more bad blood here—this tart is mad love, so much so that you won't forget or ever let go of these flavors. The buttery crust combined with a tart blood orange curd and topped with a garnish of blueberry and edible dried flowers delivers a tart bite with a sweet vengeance. And if you are new to making tarts, this recipe makes it oh so easy.

Bad Blood (Orange) Tart

Serves 8

1 recipe The Best Tart Dough (page 28)

CURD

1½ cups blood orange juice
¾ cup sugar
2 large eggs
4 egg yolks
8 tablespoons (1 stick) unsalted butter, cut into 8 pieces
Zest of 2 oranges

GARNISH

Blueberries
Edible dried flowers

1. Preheat the oven to 350°F.

2. Remove the prepared tart shell from the refrigerator. Line the shell with a 10-inch circle of parchment paper and fill with pie weights (or dried, uncooked rice or beans).

3. Par-bake the tart shell for 20 minutes. Remove the shell from the oven and let cool enough so you can remove the weights and parchment paper. Leave the oven on.

4. Gently prick the bottom and sides of the shell with a fork, then return it to the oven and bake until golden brown, 20 to 25 minutes more. Let cool completely. Turn down the oven to 325°F.

Recipe continues

5 Make the curd: Bring the blood orange juice to a boil in a medium saucepan. Lower the heat to a simmer and let the juice reduce to about ¾ cup. Remove from the heat.

6 In another medium saucepan, whisk together the sugar, eggs, and egg yolks to thoroughly combine. Slowly stream in the reduced blood orange juice, whisking constantly.

7 Add the butter and place the pan over medium heat. Cook, whisking constantly, until the curd is thickened and reaches a temperature of 185°F.

8 Strain the curd through a fine-mesh sieve placed over a medium bowl. Fold in the orange zest.

9 Pour the curd into the tart shell and smooth the surface. Place the tart pan on a baking sheet and bake for 10 minutes to set the curd.

10 Allow the tart to cool to room temperature, then refrigerate for at least 2 hours. Garnish with blueberries and edible flowers, and serve. Store covered in the refrigerator for up to 5 days.

It's (blue)berry cobbler and the feeling I got is summer. It doesn't have to be a cruel summer as long as you have a cobbler recipe to use with all the summertime blueberries in season. No blueberries? No need to be delicate about it. You can simply swap the blueberries for another seasonal fruit, like cherries or peaches. Best served warm with a scoop of ice cream on top, this cobbler is so good you won't want to share.

Never Seen That Color (Blue)berry Cobbler

Serves 12

- 2 cups fresh or frozen blueberries
- Zest of 2 lemons
- ¼ cup fresh lemon juice
- Granulated sugar
- 8 tablespoons (1 stick) unsalted butter
- 1 cup all-purpose flour, sifted
- 1½ teaspoons baking powder
- 1 teaspoon kosher salt
- ½ teaspoon pure vanilla extract
- ½ cup whole milk
- Raw sugar, for topping

1 Preheat the oven to 350°F.

2 Combine the blueberries, lemon zest, lemon juice, and 1 tablespoon granulated sugar in a medium bowl. Set aside.

3 Melt the butter in a 10-inch cast-iron skillet over low heat.

4 Whisk together the flour, ⅔ cup granulated sugar, the baking powder, and salt in a medium bowl until well incorporated. With a wooden spoon or flexible silicone spatula, stir in the vanilla and milk to create a thick batter.

5 Pour the batter over the melted butter and then top with the blueberry mixture. No need to stir; the cobbler will bake around the blueberries in the oven.

6 Bake for 15 minutes, then sprinkle raw sugar over the top. Continue baking until the cobbler is golden brown and set around the edges, 15 to 25 minutes more. Store covered in the refrigerator for up to 5 days.

Whether it's 2 a.m. in your car or in your room, this pie in a jar is a sweet treat to be enjoyed wherever. With a graham cracker crust and berry chamomile compote, you'll never forget the flavors as long as you live. You simply layer the crust and berry mixture of each pie in a 4-ounce mason jar. The recipe makes 8 pies, ensuring you'll have enough for your whole squad. And once it's gone, you'll wish it were right here, right now again because it was THAT GOOD.

Take it with you on road trips, enjoy it late at night under the covers with your lover, or if you are at home, in your room, all alone, indulge just yourself. No one is judging.

Squad Goals:

Attending a Fourth of July party? Hosting a baby shower for a friend? Bejewel the jars with celebration-appropriate ribbons, friendship bracelets, and/or mini wooden spoons and let these desserts take center stage.

It's 2 a.m. Pie in a Jar

Makes 8 jars

CRUST

- 12 graham crackers, processed into a fine crumb texture
- ¼ cup sugar
- ¾ teaspoon salt
- 6½ tablespoons melted unsalted butter

FILLING

- ½ cup sugar
- 1 chamomile tea bag
- 2 cups fresh or frozen blueberries
- ¼ cup fresh lemon juice
- 1 tablespoon cornstarch

Whipped cream or ice cream, for serving (optional)

1 **Make the crust:** Mix together the graham cracker crumbs, sugar, and salt in a medium bowl. Add the melted butter and stir until the mixture has a wet, sandy texture.

Recipe continues

2 Scoop 3 tablespoons of the mixture into the bottom of each 4-ounce mason jar. Place the jars in the refrigerator to chill.

3 **Meanwhile, make the filling:** Stir together the sugar and ½ cup water in a medium saucepan over low heat until the sugar dissolves.

4 Turn off the heat and add the chamomile tea bag. Cover and let steep for 5 minutes.

5 Remove and discard the tea bag. Add the blueberries to the saucepan and heat over medium-low heat, stirring occasionally, until some of the blueberries begin to pop, about 5 minutes.

6 Meanwhile, mix together the cornstarch and lemon juice into a slurry in a small bowl, then pour the slurry into the blueberries, stirring constantly until the mixture thickens.

7 Once the mixture bubbles, remove it from the heat and transfer to a medium bowl to cool.

8 Divide the filling equally among the chilled pie jars. Top with a dollop of whipped cream or a small scoop of ice cream, if desired. Store covered in the refrigerator for up to 5 days.

All-purpose flour, for the work surface

1 recipe Pie, Pie, Baby Dough (page 27)

FILLING

6 to 8 Granny Smith apples, quartered, cored, and sliced into ¼-inch-thick half-moons

¼ cup granulated sugar

¼ cup packed light brown sugar

4 tablespoons (½ stick) unsalted butter, melted

2 teaspoons ground cinnamon

¼ teaspoon ground cardamom

1 teaspoon kosher salt

2 tablespoons cornstarch

2 tablespoons fresh lemon juice

1½ teaspoons rose water

ASSEMBLY

Heavy cream, for brushing

Raw sugar, for sprinkling

One slice of this pie and people will be saying, "Oh my god, who is she?" That's because this apple pie is as classic as a red lip but with a rosy twist. The apples are first soaked in rose water, which infuses this traditional pie with a sweet floral undertone.

While apple pie is typically an autumn dessert, this version is perfect during an early-spring snow when it's still chilly enough to take comfort in a warm slice of pie while dreaming of the floral blooms ahead.

Rose Garden Apple Pie

Serves 8

1 Lightly flour your work surface, rolling pin, and hands. Remove one of the prepared dough disks from the refrigerator and place on the work surface (keep the other refrigerated until ready to roll). Working quickly so the dough stays cold, roll out the dough, starting from the center of the disk, into a 12-inch round. Gently turn your dough with your hands between rolls to maintain an even thickness and shape. Fit the dough into a 9-inch pie dish. Trim the edge with a small paring knife, leaving a 1-inch overhang.

2 Make the filling: Combine the apples, granulated sugar, brown sugar, melted butter, cinnamon, cardamom, and salt in a large bowl.

Recipe continues

3 Whisk together the cornstarch, lemon juice, and rose water in a small bowl until lump-free. Pour this over the apples and stir to combine. Allow the apple mixture to rest for at least 30 minutes to develop flavor, then pour the mixture into the pie shell.

4 **To assemble:** Remove the remaining disk of chilled pie dough from the refrigerator, roll it into a 12-inch round, then lay on top of the filling. Trim the excess dough, leaving a 1-inch overhang. Gently press to seal with the bottom crust, then crimp the edges.

5 Lightly brush the top of the piecrust with the heavy cream, then sprinkle the top with raw sugar. Cut small vent holes into the top of the pie. Refrigerate the pie while the oven preheats.

6 Preheat the oven to 400°F.

7 Place the pie dish on a large baking sheet and bake for 20 minutes. Reduce the oven temperature to 375°F and continue baking until the crust is golden brown and the filling juices are bubbling and thick, 60 to 70 minutes.

8 Let the pie cool completely before slicing and serving. Store covered in the refrigerator for up to 5 days.

You'll want to run as fast as you can toward these custard-style chess pie bites. The custard filling is a base of sugar, eggs, and butter with cornmeal mixed in to give it an elevated texture. The sugar from the filling caramelizes on the top, giving it a nice crispy layer. Whether you are playing chess or cards, these chess pie bites make the perfect dessert to bring to a game night with friends. Serve on a chessboard for an added touch only a mastermind could think of!

It's Nice to Have a Friend:

While this recipe calls for a mini tart tamper to press your dough out, it's okay if you don't have one! You can use a flat-bottom drinking glass, a wine cork, or even the flat end of a wooden spoon. The most important thing is to ensure you have a flat surface and an even consistency.

I Lived in Your Chess Pie Bites

Makes 24 bites

- 1 recipe The Best Tart Dough (page 28), prepared only through step 3 of that recipe
- 3 large eggs
- 1 large egg yolk
- 1 cup granulated sugar
- ½ cup packed dark brown sugar
- 8 tablespoons (1 stick) unsalted butter, melted and cool
- ½ cup buttermilk
- 1 teaspoon pure vanilla extract
- 1 tablespoon white vinegar
- 2 tablespoons finely ground cornmeal
- 1 tablespoon all-purpose flour, sifted
- ¼ teaspoon freshly grated nutmeg
- ¼ teaspoon salt

1 Using a mini tart tamper (for alternatives, see It's Nice to Have a Friend), roll 2 tablespoons of the dough into a ball. Press each ball of dough into the wells of a 12-cup mini muffin

Recipe continues

tin to create the tart shells. Place the muffin tin in the freezer for 30 minutes.

2 Remove the muffin tin from the freezer and trim any excess dough from the frozen tart shells with a sharp paring knife.

3 Preheat the oven to 400°F.

4 Bake the mini tart shells until golden brown, 8 to 10 minutes. Remove from the oven and let cool completely in the pan. Lower the oven temperature to 325°F.

5 While the shells are cooling, make the filling. Whisk together the eggs, egg yolk, and both sugars in a large bowl. Stir in the melted butter, buttermilk, vanilla, and vinegar. Add the cornmeal, flour, nutmeg, and salt and whisk well to combine.

6 Divide the filling evenly among the wells, filling each almost to the top.

7 Bake the mini pies until the tops begin to bubble, 12 to 15 minutes. Let cool completely before removing from the pan. Once cool, run a paring knife around the edges of the wells to remove the pies. Store covered in the refrigerator for up to 5 days.

Happy, free, lonely, and confused at the same time is how we describe Daisy May's Strawberry Pretzel Salad. While these flavors and textures seem to contradict each other (kind of like when midnights become your afternoons), it's also like they belong together. Can't you see? The salty crunch of the pretzel crust combined with the sweetness of the strawberry gelatin and the creaminess of the whipped cream will make this treat your new favorite. You have no reason to be afraid with this recipe. If you like, you can top with additional whipped cream, sliced strawberries, and crushed pretzel pieces.

Daisy May's Strawberry Pretzel Salad

Serves 12

CRUST

- 2 cups crushed, salted pretzels
- 1½ sticks unsalted butter, melted
- 3 tablespoons sugar

FILLING

- 1 (8-ounce) package cream cheese, softened
- 1 cup sugar
- ¼ teaspoon salt
- 2 cups heavy cream
- ¼ teaspoon cream of tartar
- 1 teaspoon pure vanilla extract
- 2 (3-ounce) packages strawberry gelatin
- 2 cups boiling water
- 4 to 5 cups frozen and thawed or fresh sliced strawberries

1 Preheat the oven to 350°F.

2 **Make the crust:** Combine the crushed pretzels, melted butter, and 3 tablespoons sugar in a medium bowl. Press into an ungreased 13 × 9-inch baking pan and bake for 10 minutes. Set aside the crust to cool.

3 **Make the filling:** Place the softened cream cheese, sugar, and salt in the bowl of a stand mixer fitted with the paddle attachment and beat on low speed, scraping down the sides of the bowl as needed, until combined and no lumps remain,

about 3 to 5 minutes. Transfer the mixture to a medium bowl. Wash and dry the mixer's bowl to use again.

4 Fit the mixer with the whip attachment and add the heavy cream, cream of tartar, and vanilla to the mixer's bowl. Whip on medium speed until the cream thickens, about 5 minutes, and then increase to high speed to achieve stiff peaks, about 7 minutes. Gently fold in the cream cheese mixture to the whipped cream until it just comes together.

5 Spoon the mixture over the cooled pretzel crust and smooth it with a flexible silicone spatula into an even layer all the way to the edges.

6 Stir together the gelatin and the boiling water in a large bowl until dissolved. Stir in the strawberries. Refrigerate this mixture until it begins to set, 10 to 15 minutes. This will make it easier to spread and less likely to bleed into the cream cheese layer.

7 Carefully spoon the strawberry gelatin on top of the cream cheese layer. Refrigerate for at least 4 hours before slicing. Store covered in the refrigerator for up to 5 days.

While it will never measure up in any measure to a traditional pecan pie, this tiny pecan pie packs a big punch in a perfectly petite package. While you could make these when spring breaks loose or during the sparkling summer months, they are best served during the fall. This is one recipe that you can slide through inboxes and DMs with your friends.

Pop-Star Tip:

Add in the zest of 1 orange along with the pecans for a bit of brightness! Or you can use edible glitter paint to paint the pecan halves to top the mini pies with.

The Smallest Pecan Pie Who Ever Lived

Makes 24 mini pies

Nonstick cooking spray

All-purpose flour, for the work surface

Pie, Pie, Baby Dough (page 27)

1 cup granulated sugar

3 tablespoons packed light brown sugar

3 large eggs

1 teaspoon salt

½ teaspoon ground cinnamon

1 cup light corn syrup

5½ tablespoons unsalted butter, melted

1 teaspoon pure vanilla extract

1½ cups pecan halves, toasted and finely chopped

24 pecan halves, toasted

1 Lightly grease the wells of two 12-cup mini muffin tins with cooking spray.

2 Lightly flour your work surface, rolling pin, and hands. Roll out the pie dough to ¼-inch thickness and cut out 2-inch-diameter rounds with a biscuit cutter. Fit the dough rounds into each cavity of the muffin tin. Gently press down, then

Recipe continues

trim any excess with a small paring knife. Place the muffin tin in the freezer for 30 minutes.

3 About 10 minutes before removing the tin from the freezer, preheat the oven to 400°F.

4 Prick the bottom of each shell with a fork, then place the tin in the oven to par-bake the shells until golden brown, 5 to 7 minutes. Let the shells cool in the muffin tin while you prepare the filling.

5 Reduce the oven temperature to 325°F.

6 Mix together both sugars, the eggs, salt, and cinnamon in a large bowl. Stir in the corn syrup, melted butter, and vanilla until well combined. Fold in the chopped pecans.

7 Distribute the filling evenly among the shells. Lightly press a pecan half on top of each "pie."

8 Bake until the filling looks set and still has a slight jiggle in the center, 10 to 15 minutes. Let cool in the tin on a wire rack, then run a paring knife around the edges of the wells to remove the pies.

Your depression will no longer be working the graveyard shift once you've enjoyed the smooth chocolate pudding and crunchy cookie bite of these chocolaty treats. The best thing about this recipe is that you can add your favorite embellishments—gummy snakes, chocolate candy rocks, and tombstones with phrases like RIP Nils Sjöberg or RIP ME. Make them extra special by serving with shovel spoons so you can dig up hatchets in the pudding and cookie layers. No map needed to start digging in and enjoying the flavors and textures of this dessert.

Three Months in the Grave Cups

Serves 8

- 1 (3.9-ounce) package chocolate instant pudding mix
- 2 cups cold whole milk
- 1 (8-ounce) container whipped topping, such as Cool Whip, thawed
- 1 (14-ounce) package chocolate sandwich cookies, such as Oreos, crushed
- Gummy snakes and chocolate rocks, for decorating (optional)

OTHER SUPPLIES
- 8 clear plastic dessert cups
- Shovel spoons (optional)

1 Whisk together the pudding mix and milk in a large bowl until thickened, about 2 minutes. Let it sit for 5 minutes to fully set.

2 Gently fold the whipped topping into the pudding until well combined.

3 To assemble the cups, place a layer of cookie crumbs at the bottom of each cup. Add a layer of the pudding mixture, then top with more cookie crumbs. Continue layering, leaving ¼-inch space at the top for decorations, if using.

Recipe continues

4 To decorate, add candy rocks or gummy snakes, or make tombstones out of Milano cookies or make your own using sugar cookies.

5 Chill the cups for at least 1 hour before serving. Serve cold, dig in with a shovel spoon, if using, and enjoy! Store covered in the refrigerator for up to 5 days.

These blue raspberry gelatin treats, offering a cool reprieve from the heat, are just what you want to dive into during the warm summer months. While the recipe is super easy, the star of the show is your choice of decorations. In this version, peach rings serve as pool floats, and the gummy bears are taking a dip. But there are so many other possibilities, too: Rainbow fruit strips can make a colorful slide, and marshmallows can be transformed into beach balls.

You can serve these treats in 8- to 10-ounce dessert glasses. Want to upgrade the recipe for a grown-up gathering? Add a few shots of Patrón and serve these gelatin treats in shot glasses.

You Need to Calm Down Pool Cups

Makes 8 pool cups

Vanilla frosting, for the dessert glass rims

Pink sugar crystal sprinkles, for the dessert glass rims

1 (6-ounce family-size) package berry blue gelatin dessert

1 Coat the rims of the dessert glasses with frosting with your finger.

2 Place sprinkles on a plate and dip the frosted edges into the sprinkles. Refrigerate the dessert glasses.

3 Prepare the gelatin dessert as directed on the package. Use a funnel or measuring cup to slowly pour the gelatin in the glasses, leaving a little room at the top. Refrigerate for 4 hours.

4 Once the gelatin has completely set, you can decorate as you see fit. Keep refrigerated until ready to serve. Store covered in the refrigerator for up to 5 days.

PASTRIES THAT LOOK LIKE DRESSES

Danishes, Croissants, Pretzels, and Other Pastries

Eating a pastry shaped like a gown? With a selection of danishes, croissants, pretzels, and éclairs, there are plenty of options to match your pastry with a dress you have in your closet. One look and you'll be saying, "Let's eat now."

The best day(nish)es are ones you get to share and enjoy with family and friends. Sure, fancy award parties and dinners are great, but spending time with the people you love is what matters most. Even Taylor, one of the busiest people in the world, always makes time to hang out with her family and her squad, and she even visits local children's hospitals in her downtime. This caring queen knows the importance of connection.

These day(nish)es are the perfect treat for an afternoon brunch with friends. Going window-shopping or antiquing with your mom or another loved one? Pack a few for the road!

The Best Day(nish)

Makes 16 danishes

All-purpose flour, for the work surface

Pastry Dough (page 30)

2 (8-ounce) packages cream cheese

½ cup sugar

1 large egg

½ teaspoon pure vanilla extract

⅛ teaspoon salt

Fresh fruit, like peaches or apricots, sliced ¼ inch thick, or blueberries

1 large egg, whisked for egg wash, for finishing

1 Lightly flour your work surface, then turn out the dough. Roll out the dough into a 10 × 10-inch square. Remove the butter from the parchment and place it on top of the dough. Fold the dough over to enclose the butter. Roll out the dough into an 8 × 24-inch rectangle, then fold the dough in thirds, like a letter. Rotate the dough 90 degrees and repeat the process two more times. Wrap the dough in plastic wrap and refrigerate for 1 hour.

2 Line two baking sheets with parchment paper. Remove the dough from the refrigerator and roll out into an 8 × 24-inch rectangle. Cut the dough into sixteen 3 × 4-inch rectangles and place them on the prepared baking sheets. Cover with plastic wrap and let proof in a warm place until doubled in size and the layers begin to separate. Start checking after 1 hour, and then in 30-minute intervals until proofed.

3 Preheat the oven to 400°F.

4 **Make the filling:** Place the cream cheese, sugar, egg, vanilla, and salt in the bowl of the stand mixer fitted with the paddle attachment and mix on low speed, scraping down the sides of the bowl as needed, until combined, 5 to 7 minutes.

5 Brush the tops gently with egg wash. Scoop or pipe the filling on top of the danishes and adorn with fruit before baking.

6 Bake for 10 to 15 minutes, then reduce the oven temperature to 325°F and continue baking until the filling is set and the pastry is golden brown, 25 minutes more. Keep a close eye on them so they don't burn. Store covered in the refrigerator for up to 5 days.

Taylor's hometown of Reading, Pennsylvania, is known as the "Pretzel Capital of the U.S.," as it was once home to more than two dozen pretzel factories and the city where the first automated pretzel twisting machine was invented.

There's something about a mall pretzel that feels so high school, like before there was the internet. From the comfort of your own kitchen, allow yourself to slip back into a moment in time when you walked past the food court inhaling that buttery, twisted-dough goodness. If you really want to create that true mall pretzel feel at home, twist the pretzel in paper sheets (like parchment paper) and pretend you are walking around the mall with friends. Top your homemade pretzel with classic salt or cinnamon sugar—either choice is golden. Pair your salted pretzel with mustard or ranch, or enjoy as is.

Meet Me Behind the Mall Pretzel

Makes 6 pretzels

- Nonstick cooking spray
- 1½ cups warm whole milk
- 2¼ teaspoons instant yeast
- 3 tablespoons packed light brown sugar
- 3 cups bread flour, sifted, plus more for the work surface
- 3 tablespoons unsalted butter, melted, plus 3 tablespoons unsalted butter, melted, if making cinnamon sugar pretzels
- 1 teaspoon kosher salt
- ¼ cup baking soda
- 2½ cups warm water
- ¾ teaspoon pretzel salt (optional)
- 2 cups sugar mixed with 2 tablespoons cinnamon and ½ teaspoon table salt (optional)

1 Grease a large bowl with cooking spray and set aside.

2 Place the warm milk, yeast, and brown sugar in the bowl of a stand mixer fitted with the dough attachment and mix on low speed until frothy, about 1 minute, or until the yeast is dissolved. Gradually add the flour and 3 tablespoons of the

Recipe continues

melted butter, mixing until the dough forms a mass, 3 to 5 minutes.

3 Add the kosher salt and knead on low speed until the dough is smooth but still slightly tacky and pulls away from the sides of the bowl, about 5 minutes.

4 Shape the dough into a ball, place in the greased bowl, and cover with plastic wrap. Let rise in a warm spot until doubled in size, about 2 hours.

5 Preheat the oven to 450°F. Line a large baking sheet with parchment paper and spray lightly with cooking spray.

6 Stir together the baking soda and warm water in a 3-quart baking dish until the baking soda is dissolved.

7 Lightly flour the work surface, then turn out the dough. Cut the dough into 6 equal pieces; cover these pieces with plastic wrap while you roll out each pretzel rope.

8 Roll and stretch each piece of dough with the clean palms of your hands into a 24-inch rope. Gently dip each rope into the baking soda solution. Let any excess liquid drip off, then pick up both ends so the dough forms a U shape. Criss-cross left over right, then fold the dough down and adhere each end to the opposite side of the dough.

9 If you'd like traditional salted pretzels, sprinkle the tops with pretzel salt now. If you want a cinnamon sugar topping, bake the pretzels plain and top later.

10 Bake the pretzels until golden, 10 to 12 minutes. Remove from the oven. If making cinnamon sugar pretzels, immediately brush the tops with the remaining 3 tablespoons melted butter and sprinkle with the cinnamon sugar mixture.

All-purpose flour, for the work surface

Pastry Dough (page 30)

FILLING

½ cup confectioners' sugar

3 tablespoons butter, softened

1½ (7-ounce) tubes almond paste, room temperature

1 teaspoon salt

1 large egg white

1 teaspoon pure vanilla extract

½ teaspoon almond extract

FINISHING

1 large egg, whisked for egg wash

Raw sugar, for sprinkling

Sliced almonds, for sprinkling

Who's afraid of little old wheat? Well, you should be because this yeast and wheat pastry is so good, you'll want seconds or thirds or hundredths.

Even though it has a scary name, the pastry itself is pretty tame and gentle. It has a light, raised exterior and a rich almond-and-raisin filling that is exposed through cut-out "claws" in the dough.

This recipe is one of the more time-consuming ones (requiring a full day for the dough to rest), so once you make it, go ahead and give off a valiant roar in celebration. You deserve it!

And You'll Poke That Bear Claw

Makes 12 bear claws

1 Lightly flour your work surface, then turn out the dough. Roll out the dough into a 10 × 10-inch square. Remove the butter from the parchment and place on top of the dough. Fold the dough over to enclose the butter. Roll out the dough into an 8 × 24-inch rectangle, then fold the dough in thirds, like a letter. Rotate the dough 90 degrees and repeat the process two more times. Wrap the dough in plastic wrap and refrigerate for 1 hour.

Recipe continues

2 Meanwhile, make the filling: Place the confectioners' sugar and butter in the bowl of the stand mixer fitted with the paddle attachment (or into a large bowl if using a handheld mixer) and beat on low speed. Once it starts coming together, 2 to 3 minutes, add the almond paste, torn into pieces, and the salt and continue beating until smooth, 2 to 3 minutes. Add the egg white and the vanilla and almond extracts and beat, scraping down the sides of the bowl as needed, until combined and smooth, 2 to 3 minutes. Transfer to a piping bag fitted with a round piping tip (Ateco #803).

3 Line a large baking sheet with parchment paper and set aside.

4 Remove the dough from the refrigerator and roll out into an 8 × 24-inch square. Cut the dough into twelve 4 × 4-inch squares, then pipe a strip of filling in the center of each square. Brush the edges of the squares with water and fold in half.

5 Cut four 1-inch slits in the folded/filled side of each pastry with the seam side facing away from you. These are your "claws."

6 Place the pastries on the prepared baking sheet and gently curve the pastry to expose the claw shape.

7 Proof the pastries in a warm place until they double in size, about 60 minutes.

8 Preheat the oven to 400°F.

9 Brush the tops of the pastries with the egg wash. Sprinkle with raw sugar and sliced almonds.

10 Bake until golden brown, 18 to 20 minutes.

That's the thing about these illicit éclairs—while they are so beautiful and delicious, they also feel a bit sinful. This pastry uses choux dough, which has a high moisture content, so when baked, the water evaporates and the pastry puffs up—no yeast needed! Filled with pastry cream and topped with chocolate ganache, these decadent treats will give you a mercurial high for weeks.

These are best made with some helping hands, so you and your squad can share in the process.

Pop-Star Tip:

While éclairs are usually topped with chocolate ganache, you can top these with colorful royal icing instead and decorate with sprinkles, edible flowers, or edible glitter to give the éclairs a special shimmer.

Illicit Éclairs

Makes 8 éclairs

- 1 recipe Choux Dough (page 29)
- 2 cups milk
- 1 vanilla bean, halved and insides scraped
- ⅔ cup sugar
- 6 large egg yolks
- ¼ cup cornstarch
- 2 tablespoons cold unsalted butter
- ½ cup heavy cream
- ½ cup dark chocolate chips

1 Preheat the oven to 425°F. Line a large baking sheet with parchment paper.

2 Transfer the dough to a pastry bag fitted with a large round piping tip (Ateco #829). Pipe 4-inch-long lines of dough onto the prepared baking sheet, leaving 2 inches between each.

3 Bake for 15 minutes, then reduce the oven temperature to 375°F and continue baking until puffed and golden brown,

Recipe continues

20 to 25 minutes. Remove from the oven and, using a sharp knife, immediately poke two holes in the bottom of the pastry shells to release steam. Transfer the shells to a wire rack to cool completely.

4 While the pastry shells are cooling, make the pastry cream. Bring the milk, vanilla bean, and ⅓ cup of the sugar to a simmer in a medium saucepan, then remove from the heat.

5 Whisk together the yolks, the remaining ⅓ cup sugar, and the cornstarch in a medium bowl. While whisking, very slowly stream in the hot milk mixture—you want to temper the yolks, not scramble them.

6 Pour the mixture back into the saucepan and cook over low heat, stirring constantly, until the cream begins to thicken and bubble. Immediately remove from the heat and strain through a fine-mesh sieve into a clean medium bowl. Add the cold butter and stir until melted. Cover the bowl and refrigerate the pastry cream until cool, at least 1 hour.

7 Remove the pastry cream from the refrigerator and whisk until smooth. Transfer the cream to a piping bag fitted with a donut-filling tip (#230 bismark). Pipe the cream into the holes until the éclairs feel full. Set aside while you make the glaze.

8 Heat the heavy cream in a small saucepan over medium heat until it just starts to bubble and steam. (Alternatively, place the heavy cream in a medium microwave-safe bowl and heat on high temperature for 15- to 30-second intervals, checking after each interval, until melted.) Add the chocolate and let the mixture stand for 2 minutes. Then gently whisk until melted and smooth. Dip the tops of the eclairs in the warm chocolate glaze and set them on a small baking sheet.

9 Refrigerate the éclairs, uncovered, for at least 1 hour to set the glaze, or keep refrigerated until ready to enjoy. Store covered in the refrigerator for up to 5 days.

The thrill of making these churros does not expire. After all, fried dough wrapped in a cozy cardigan of sugar and served with a side of chocolate sauce? What's not to love?

While these are easy to make, they do require frying, so open windows and turn on fans to vent your kitchen. But after one bite, you'll have a new favorite recipe that you'll want to make again and again.

Chasing Churros in the Grocery Line

Makes 6 to 8 churros

2 cups sugar

2 tablespoons ground cinnamon

¼ teaspoon salt

1 gallon vegetable oil

1 recipe Choux Dough (page 29)

Dipping sauce (optional)

1. Line a plate with paper towels and set aside.

2. Mix the sugar, cinnamon, and salt in a shallow bowl or pie dish and set aside.

3. Heat the oil to 370°F in a large stockpot.

4. Transfer the dough to a pastry bag fitted with a large star piping tip (Ateco #847). Carefully pipe the dough in 6-inch lengths into the hot oil, using scissors to trim the end off of each churro while piping.

5. Fry until golden brown, about 1 minute, then flip and fry the other side for another minute. Using tongs, carefully transfer the fried churros to the lined plate for about 30 seconds.

6. Toss the churros in sugar mixture, shake off the excess, and serve hot, with sauce, if desired. These are best enjoyed within 24 hours.

Seeing the incandescent glow when taking these pains au chocolat out of the oven—there is no better feeling. It's like you are eating one straight from a Parisian boulangerie. The buttery, flaky layers with the gooey chocolate interior fits perfectly in the palm of your hand, but it won't last long there.

Perfect to warm you up when coming in from the snow or during the early-spring months when clover starts to bloom. This is one pastry that is truly timeless. Best enjoyed warm.

My Pain au Chocolat Fits in the Palm of Your Freezing Hand

Makes 8 pains au chocolat

All-purpose flour, for the work surface

Pastry Dough (page 30)

1 (12-ounce) bag mini dark chocolate chips or 16 chocolate batons

EGG WASH

1 large egg

¼ cup heavy cream

1 Lightly flour your work surface, then turn out the dough. Roll out the dough into a 10 × 10-inch square. Remove the butter from the parchment and place on top of the dough. Fold the dough over to enclose the butter. Roll out the dough into an 8 × 24-inch rectangle, then fold the dough into thirds, like a letter. Rotate the dough 90 degrees and repeat the process two more times. Wrap the dough in plastic wrap and refrigerate for 1 hour.

Recipe continues

2 Line two baking sheets with parchment paper. Remove the dough from the refrigerator and roll out into an 8 × 24-inch rectangle. Cut the dough into eight 4 × 6-inch rectangles. With the narrow end facing you, place a line of the mini chocolate chips at the top of the dough and roll the dough toward you so the chips are encased in dough. (If using French chocolate batons, set one baton per rectangle.) Place another line (or baton) on the dough and roll the dough to encase the chocolate and form a cylinder. Transfer the croissants to the prepared baking sheets.

3 Whisk together the egg and heavy cream in a small bowl. Brush the egg wash over the croissants, gently cover with plastic wrap, and proof in a warm place until double in size, 2 to 6 hours. Reserve the remaining egg wash.

4 Preheat the oven to 425°F.

5 Give the egg wash another whisk and brush it over the croissants one more time before baking.

6 Bake for 10 minutes, then reduce the oven temperature to 325°F and bake for another 20 to 25 minutes, until golden brown.

When they point to the dessert tray, please tell them the name: madeleines. Part cookie, part cake, these seashell-shaped treats have a sponge cake consistency but are small enough to snack on a few with a cup of coffee or hot cocoa. They typically have a citrus zest and are sometimes dusted with confectioners' sugar, but they can also be made with a chocolate chip–infused batter.

While the chocolate chip addition can be a fun touch every once in a while, you'll likely be saying, "I love you just the way you were," since the classic version is Mr. Perfectly Fine.

These are best enjoyed the day they are baked!

Pop-Star Tip:

This recipe requires a special madeleine pan to give these treats their signature seashell shape, so make sure you have one on hand before beginning.

Chloe or Sam or Sophia or Madeleines

Makes 16 madeleines

- ½ cup plus 1½ tablespoons all-purpose flour, sifted
- ¼ cup plus 2 tablespoons sugar
- ½ teaspoon baking powder
- ¼ teaspoon kosher salt
- 2 large eggs
- 5½ teaspoons pure vanilla extract
- 5 tablespoons unsalted butter, melted, plus more for greasing

OTHER SUPPLIES

16-cavity madeleine mold

1 Whisk together the flour, sugar, baking powder, and salt in a medium bowl. Add the eggs and vanilla, whisking until a thick batter forms. Whisk in the melted butter until fully incorporated and the batter is smooth and shiny.

Recipe continues

2   Cover the batter and refrigerate for at least 4 hours before baking.

3   Preheat the oven to 425°F.

4   Using a pastry brush, grease a madeleine pan with some melted butter. Place the pan in the freezer for 30 minutes.

5   Using a 1-tablespoon cookie scoop or measuring spoon, drop the batter into each cavity of the prepared madeleine pan.

6   Bake for 5 minutes, then reduce the oven temperature to 400°F and continue baking until the madeleines are domed in the center and golden brown around the edges, 8 to 10 minutes.

7   Remove the pan from the oven and immediately invert onto a wire rack to release the madeleines from the mold. Cool completely. Flip the madeleines right side up and serve.

What do you get when a pop star (Taylor Swift) and one of the most famous and beloved chefs of all time (Ina Garten) get together to bake? A gorgeous pavlova. A pavlova is a gluten-free, meringue-based dessert that is crispy on the outside but soft and fluffy on the inside. While typically made to look like a cake, these pretty pavlovas are individually portioned to make it easier to share with your entire squad. Topped with fresh berries and edible flowers, your guests will truly feel like the lucky one with this dessert.

Everybody Loves Pretty Pavlova

Makes 4 (3-inch) pavlovas

- 5 large egg whites, room temperature
- 1 cup sugar
- 1 teaspoon cream of tartar (to stabilize the meringue)
- 1 teaspoon cornstarch (to keep the meringue soft inside after baking)
- ½ teaspoon salt
- 1½ teaspoons pure vanilla extract
- 1 (4-ounce) carton blueberries
- 1 (4-ounce) carton strawberries
- 1 (4-ounce) package ready-to-eat pomegranate seeds
- Edible flowers (optional)

1 Preheat the oven to 225°F. Line a baking sheet with parchment paper, draw four 3-inch circles on the paper with a permanent marker, then flip the paper over. Set aside.

2 Bring a couple of inches of water to a simmer in a medium pot and set a medium heat-safe bowl on top of it to create a double boiler. Place the egg whites and sugar in the bowl and whisk until the sugar dissolves and the mixture reaches 170°F. Transfer the mixture to the bowl of a stand mixer fitted with the whisk attachment and whip on medium speed until medium peaks form, 3 to 5 minutes.

3 Increase the mixer speed to high. Add the cream of tartar, cornstarch, and salt and beat until stiff peaks form, scraping down the sides of the bowl as necessary, 4 to 5 minutes. Add

Recipe continues

the vanilla, mixing to incorporate. The meringue should be stiff, fluffy, and marshmallow-like.

4 Place the meringue in a piping bag fitted with a star tip (Ateco #858). Fill the center of each 3-inch circle to create a base. Then pipe on the outer edge of the base, two times around, to create a border that's higher than the base. The cavity will be about ¾ inch deep.

5 Bake the pavlovas for 1 hour, until the outside is dry. Turn off the oven and let the pavlovas cool completely in the oven with the door closed (this method prevents cracking).

6 Once completely cool, adorn with berries and edible flowers to your preference. Store pavlovas covered in the refrigerator for up to 5 days.

You know you're good when you can make these rice pops with a broken heart or anytime you're feeling down bad for a sweet treat.

While these sweet and gooey treats can be cut out in squares and served the traditional way, this recipe adds a little sequin sparkle shimmer to them by using a heart-shaped cookie cutter and candy melts and sprinkles to drizzle and decorate with. Make these treats for a friend going through a breakup, for a birthday celebration, or anytime you need a pick-me-up.

I Can Make It with a Broken Heart Crispy Rice Pops

Makes 8 to 10 pops

3 tablespoons unsalted butter, plus more for greasing

5½ cups mini marshmallows

6 cups crispy rice cereal

1 cup candy melts (choose your favorite colors)

Sprinkles

OTHER SUPPLIES

Heart-shaped cookie cutter

6 to 10 Popsicle or lollipop sticks

1 Grease a 13 × 9-inch baking pan with butter. Line a baking sheet with parchment paper. Set both aside.

2 Melt the butter in a large pot over low heat. Add the marshmallows and stir constantly until fully melted and smooth. Remove the pot from the heat and gently fold in the cereal until evenly coated.

3 Using a rubber spatula or greased hands, press the mixture into the prepared baking pan. Flatten the top evenly. Set aside for about 30 minutes to cool.

Recipe continues

4 Once set, remove the treats from the pan. Use the cookie cutter to cut out fun heart shapes.

5 Gently insert a Popsicle stick into the base of each heart and set the pops on the prepared baking sheet.

6 Place the candy melts in a small microwave-safe bowl and heat on high in 15- to 30-second intervals, checking and stirring after each interval, until melted.

7 Working with one at a time, hold a pop by the stick and dip it into the melted candy, covering about two-thirds of the heart. Lay the pop back on the baking sheet and quickly decorate the dipped portion with sprinkles before the candy hardens. Reheat the candy melt if the candy hardens before you finish decorating.

8 Let the pops set completely before serving, about 15 minutes at room temperature or 5 minutes in the refrigerator.

JUNIOR JEWELS

Candies and Other Confections

What you're looking for has been here the whole time! This section includes extra candies and confections like peanut brittle, buckeye treats, and chocolate bark. So unique, you'll want to capture your creation with a photo.

This ever-lovely jewel "candy" bracelet skewer will have you saying, "Hey, isn't this easy?" Simply place fruit, marshmallows, and candy on a skewer and use an edible pen to write your favorite friendship bracelet sayings—a perfect statement piece to bring to your next par-tay.

Squad Goals:
Have your friends over and set up a station where each guest gets to make their own unique candy bracelets.

Junior Jewels Candy Friendship Bracelet

Makes as many as you like

Fruit, such as berries, grapes, or whatever you prefer

Marshmallows

OTHER SUPPLIES

Bamboo skewers

Edible pens

1 Place the bamboo skewers in a shallow pan of water for a few minutes to keep them from splintering when skewering.

2 Skewer your fruit. Firm berries and grapes are great choices for a "bead" look.

3 The marshmallows are your "letter beads." Use an edible pen to write your message on the marshmallows, then add the marshmallows to the skewer, followed by more fruit.

4 Take a picture of your creation so you can remember it long after it's gone! Serve immediately.

Whether you grew up going to arcades on Coney Island or at a local spot in your town, this recipe guarantees you win an arcade ring every single time. Simply gather your favorite fruit juice (or juices), pour it in a jewel-shape mold, and let it freeze. Perfect for summer nights when the sun goes down, and you are ready for a cool, sweet treat.

Pop-Star Tip:

No ring mold? No problem. You can use disposable 3-ounce cups or even a muffin tin lined with foil cupcake wrappers and Popsicle sticks.

Arcade Ring Popsicles

Serves 24

32 ounces fruit juice of your choice (you can also get creative and combine flavors like strawberry and lemonade, or cherry and lime)

OTHER SUPPLIES

4 Ring Pop molds with six (1.25-ounce) rings each

1 Pour the juice into your ring pop molds. Insert Popsicle sticks into the molds, ensuring they are centered and will stand upright.

2 Place the molds in the freezer and allow the Popsicles to freeze completely (overnight is best).

3 Once fully frozen, gently remove the Popsicles from their molds. If you need to, run the molds briefly under warm water to loosen the Popsicles, but only for a second or two! Store in the freezer for up to 3 months.

You'll feel like a fearless leader after making these creamy fudge treats—just be sure you have a candy thermometer on hand. Once you get the chocolate version down bad, you'll be eager to try more variations—like adding nuts or edible glitter!

Squad Goals:

Assemble the fudge in a cute tin, use a keychain as the name tag, and gift one to a powerful woman in your life.

Fudge the Patriarchy

Serves 24

Nonstick cooking spray
3 cups sugar
⅔ cup Dutch-process cocoa powder
½ teaspoon salt
1½ cups whole milk
4 tablespoons (½ stick) unsalted butter, softened
1 teaspoon vanilla
2 cups finely chopped walnuts
Edible glitter, for dusting (optional)

1 Line an 8 × 8-inch baking pan with parchment paper and coat with cooking spray. Set aside.

2 Combine the sugar, cocoa, and salt in a medium saucepan, then add the milk and bring to a boil over medium heat, stirring, for 5 to 10 minutes. Reduce the heat a bit and place a candy thermometer in the pot. Cook the mixture until it reaches 234°F. You do not want to agitate the pot during this time. Just let it cook and get to temp without disturbing it.

3 Remove the pot from the heat and add in the butter and vanilla. Do not stir.

Recipe continues

4 Cool to 110°F.

5 Once cool, beat the mixture in the pot with a wooden spoon or rubber spatula until the shine begins to disappear. Fold in 1½ cups of the walnuts.

6 Spread the fudge quickly and evenly into the prepared pan. Top with the remaining ½ cup walnuts (if you desire, dust with edible glitter). Let cool completely (preferably overnight) at room temperature before slicing.

This peanut brittle will make you want to cozy up next to a fire with someone you love with a cup of hot cocoa in hand. While this stovetop recipe calls for just a few simple ingredients, remember that it can't take the heat too high, so it's key to have a thermometer at the ready.

I'll Keep Your Peanut Brittle Heart Warm

Serves 12 to 16 pieces

2 cups sugar

1 cup light corn syrup

2 cups salted roasted peanuts

2 tablespoons butter

1½ teaspoons baking soda

1½ teaspoons pure vanilla extract

¼ teaspoon salt

1 Line a sheet pan with parchment paper or a silicone baking mat. Set aside.

2 Attach a candy thermometer to a medium pot. Add the sugar, corn syrup, and ½ cup of water and bring to a boil over medium heat, stirring occasionally, until the temperature reaches 250°F.

3 Add the peanuts and stir the mixture constantly until the candy thermometer temperature reaches 300°F. Remove the mixture from the heat and immediately stir in the butter, baking soda, vanilla, and salt. The mixture will foam up.

4 Carefully pour the hot mixture onto the prepared sheet pan and carefully spread it into an even layer. Let cool completely before breaking apart to eat.

5 Store the completely cooled peanut brittle in an airtight container at room temperature for up to 2 weeks. Or package it up in a cute tin to share with friends.

We all know that Taylor loves her numerology. Whether it's April 29, July 9, or December 13, there is always a reason or day to celebrate, and these treats make those celebrations a little more fun. If you are in a time crunch, these date bites are the perfect way to serve something sweet in a matter of minutes. No baking required! Make and serve immediately or chill and serve later.

Do You Really Want to Know What I Ate April 29?

Makes 20 date bites

10 Medjool dates, halved and pitted

½ cup almond butter

½ cup dark chocolate chips

Flaky sea salt, such as Maldon, for topping

1 Line a baking sheet with parchment paper. Arrange the date halves on the baking sheet and spoon a little almond butter into each of the halves.

2 Bring a couple of inches of water to a simmer in a small pot and set a small heat-safe bowl on top of it to create a double boiler. Place the chocolate in the bowl and stir until melted. (Alternatively, place the chocolate in a small microwave-safe bowl and heat on high for 20-second intervals, checking at each interval, until melted.)

3 Drizzle the melted chocolate over the dates and top with a sprinkling of flaky sea salt. Store covered in the refrigerator for up to 5 days.

The perfect movie-night treat, these cookie dough bites are reminiscent of the ones you would find in a vending machine or movie theater concession stand. While that version is typically made with chocolate chips, this one uses confetti sprinkles to keep the night sparkling, no matter what.

Whether you are hosting a Sunday matinee or an evening screening of Miss Americana *or* Taylor Swift: The Eras Tour, *grab some popcorn, make these cookie dough bites, and get lost in the film.*

Vending Machine Cookie Dough Bites

Makes 22 bites

- ½ cup creamy almond or peanut butter
- ⅓ cup pure maple syrup
- ½ tablespoon pure vanilla extract
- 1 cup almond or cashew flour
- ¼ cup confetti sprinkles

1 Line a baking sheet with parchment and set aside.

2 Mix together the nut butter, maple syrup, and vanilla until well incorporated. Add the flour and continue mixing until a ball of smooth dough forms. Mix in the sprinkles.

3 Roll the dough into bite-size balls and place on the prepared baking sheet. Transfer the baking sheet to the freezer for 30 minutes before serving. Enjoy! Store covered in the refrigerator for up to 5 days.

All the pieces (dark chocolate chips, salted pretzels, banana chips, coconut flakes, and almonds) fall right into place, making the perfect chocolate bark for an afternoon treat or a 2 a.m. snack. While it makes a batch of about a dozen, you'll feel like there's never enough once you've had one taste.

It's a 2 a.m. Surprise!

The best part about this recipe is that you can swap whatever ingredients you'd like for something you like even more.

And All the Chocolate Pieces Fall Right into Place Bark

Makes about 12 pieces

- 2 (10-ounce) bags dark chocolate chips, melted
- ½ cup chopped salted pretzels
- ¼ cup chopped dried banana chips
- ¼ cup sweetened coconut flakes
- ¼ cup chopped or whole toasted peanuts or almonds
- Flaky sea salt, such as Maldon, for topping

1 Line a baking sheet with parchment paper or a silicone baking mat. Pour a third of the melted chocolate onto the prepared baking sheet and use a spatula to spread it into an even layer.

2 Evenly sprinkle with half the pretzels, banana chips, coconut, and nuts. Pour over the remaining melted chocolate and spread evenly over the top. Evenly sprinkle the remaining pretzels, banana chips, coconut, and nuts, then top with some flaky salt.

3 Allow the bark to cool until completely set, then break into pieces.

Please picture these buckeye treats inspired by the buckeye tree: A small peanut ball is peeking out from a layer of chocolate, resembling the tree's nut. While similar to a peanut butter cup, these contrarian treats contain more peanut butter than chocolate.

Long Story Short:

These treats can be frozen inside a glass storage container and enjoyed cold, too!

You're My Best Friend Buckeyes

Makes 14 to 16 buckeyes

- 1 cup creamy peanut butter
- 3 tablespoons unsalted butter
- 2 cups confectioners' sugar, sifted
- 1 teaspoon pure vanilla extract
- 2 cups semi-sweet chocolate chips
- 2 tablespoons shortening or coconut oil

1 Place the peanut butter, butter, and confectioners' sugar in the bowl of a stand mixer fitted with the paddle attachment and mix on low speed, scraping down the sides of the bowl as needed, until combined. Add the vanilla and mix in.

2 Pinch off the dough by the tablespoonful, shape into balls, and place on a baking sheet. Place the baking sheet in the refrigerator to chill for at least 30 minutes and up to an hour.

3 Meanwhile, bring a couple of inches of water to a simmer in a medium pot and set a medium heat-safe bowl on top of it to create a double boiler. Place the chocolate and coconut oil in the bowl and stir until melted and smooth. (Alternatively, place the chocolate and coconut oil in a microwave-safe medium bowl and heat on high for 15- to 30-second intervals, checking and stirring after each interval, until melted.) Let cool slightly.

4   Using a skewer or toothpick, dip the peanut butter balls into the chocolate mixture. Leave a bit of the peanut butter exposed for that signature buckeye nut look.

5   Return the buckeyes to the refrigerator until you are ready to enjoy. Store covered in the refrigerator for up to 5 days.

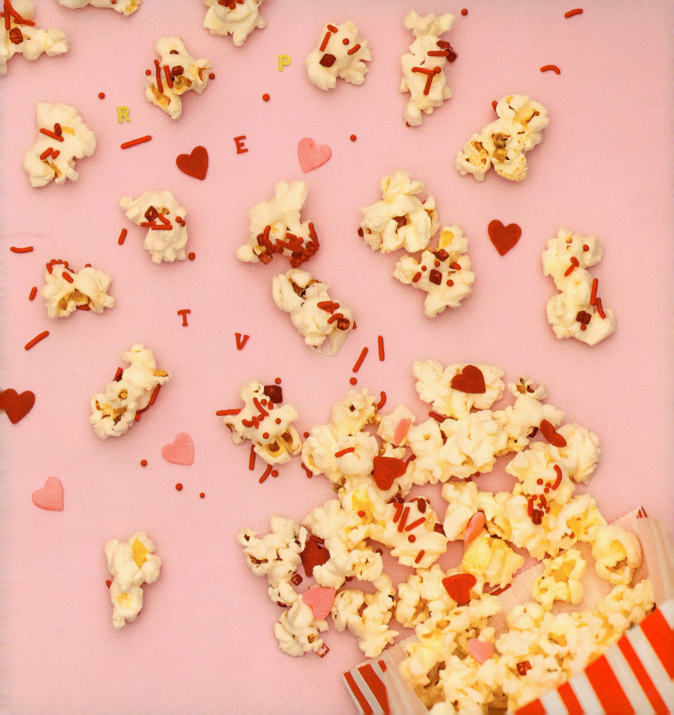

This simple popcorn recipe provides both sweet (think sweet tea in the summer) and salty (like the ocean air in August). Combined, this is a pairing that you surely won't forget anytime soon.

You can use either dark or white chocolate (or both!) and top with your favorite colorful sprinkles. Serve in individual cups and share with friends. While the popcorn is best enjoyed fresh out of the microwave, you can store it in an airtight container for 1 to 2 days.

If you are hosting a movie night with friends, set up a popcorn station with special popcorn bags so your friends feel like they are actually at the movies. This fun touch will go a long way in creating extra-special memories with those you love.

Rep Going Down Popcorn

Makes 3 to 4 cups

1 bag microwavable salted popcorn

⅔ cup white or dark chocolate

Sprinkles, for topping

1. Line a baking sheet with parchment paper.

2. Prepare the popcorn as directed on the bag. Once fully popped, spread it out on the baking sheet. Set aside.

3. Place the chocolate in a small microwave-safe bowl and heat on high for 15-second intervals, checking and stirring after each interval, until melted.

4. Drizzle the chocolate over the popcorn with a spoon. Add sprinkles and let set for about 15 minutes. Serve immediately.

"What's your favorite Taylor Swift album?" If you are like me, it changes on a daily basis depending on what's going on in my life and my general mood. Do I want to feel uplifted like I'm "The Man"? Do I want to cry in the back of a car over a breakup? Am I in my vigilante shit era and secretly seeking revenge? Am I feeling nostalgic for Taylor's debut album? Just when I think I have a favorite, a memory of another song from another album that I love so much comes on and I'm back to square one.

This milkshake was inspired by that inability to pick just one! There are layers of Lover, 1989, and Midnights swirled in the colors, textures, and display of this milkshake. Want some Red vibes? Swap the vanilla ice cream for red velvet or add some food coloring. Leaning more toward Speak Now? Add purple cotton candy to the shake. No matter what era you're feeling, you can make your milkshake to match!

Midnight Lover Shake, Shake, Shake!

Serves 2

- 2 cups vanilla ice cream, plus more as needed
- 1 cup whole milk, plus more as needed
- 1 cup cotton candy, plus more for garnish
- ½ teaspoon pure vanilla extract (optional but nice for a flavor boost)
- Pink or blue food coloring (optional but nice for an extra pop of color)
- Frosting, for the glass rim
- Sprinkles, for the glass rim and topping

1 Blend the vanilla ice cream, milk, cotton candy, and vanilla, if using, in a blender until smooth. Add a drop or two of food coloring, if desired, for a fun cotton candy hue. If the milkshake is too thick, add a splash of milk and blend again. If it's too thin, add more ice cream.

2 Brush the rim of your glass with frosting and dip it into a plate of sprinkles. Pour the milkshake into the glass and top with a puff of cotton candy and some sprinkles. Serve immediately.

Taylor loves writing handwritten letters and sending care packages to her fans. In 2014, December was dubbed "Swiftmas," after Taylor bought gifts for fans. She not only gift-wrapped them herself and included a personal letter, but in some cases, she even hand-delivered them. More recently, she wrote handwritten thank-you notes to her truck drivers on the Eras Tour and gifted everyone with a $100,000 bonus.

While you might not have an extra $100K to give, a small gift of treats and a handwritten note can go a long way toward letting someone know you are thinking about them. It's the perfect little pick-me-up that will have them feeling better than they ever were.

Yes, I Got Your Letter (with Candy!)

Serves 1

- Your favorite candy that you love to share
- Letter and envelope
- Box or package, for delivery or shipping

1. Gather a selection of your favorite candies—gummies, chocolates, sour hard candies, Squashies, or whatever you think your recipient would most enjoy.

2. Write a letter to your friend and let them know you are thinking about them and want to sweeten their day with some of your favorite treats.

3. Package up the candies and your note and either send through the mail or hand-deliver the goods.

Just like a mirrorball, these dipped marshmallows can show you everything... about what your favorite flavors are. While this is a very simple recipe, it allows you to cater to all the different versions of yourself— the one who likes sweet, the one who likes salty, the one who likes creamy, and the one who likes crunchy. Be sure to have skewers or lollipop sticks on hand.

Par=tay Tip:

A fun hosting option is to display assorted toppings in mini fondue pots and let guests choose what they like. You can also wrap these mirrorball treats individually in cellophane, tie them with some cute ribbon, and gift them at parties.

Mirrorball Marshmallows

Makes 10 to 15 mirrorballs

10 to 15 large marshmallows

Sprinkles, crushed nuts, cookies, and/or crushed cookies, for toppings

1 cup semi-sweet, milk, or white chocolate or colored candy melts

Lollipop sticks or skewers

1 Line a baking sheet with parchment paper. Insert a skewer or lollipop stick into each marshmallow and set on the prepared baking sheet.

2 Arrange your toppings in small individual bowls. Set aside.

3 Place the chocolate or candy melts in a small microwave-safe bowl and heat on high for 15- to 30-second intervals, checking and stirring after each interval, until fully melted.

4 Dip the marshmallow into the chocolate and cover either halfway or completely.

5 Immediately coat your chocolate-covered marshmallows with your preferred toppings.

6 Return the marshmallows to the baking sheet and let sit at room temperature for 15 minutes or until the chocolate or candy melts completely harden. These are best enjoyed they day they're made.

BONUS
KITTY CAKES AND DOG BONES

We can't forget about treats for our favorite furry friends!

One nibble of this cake and your cat will be purring in your lap because they love you so much for making this extra-special birthday cake. A purrrrfect cake to celebrate your cat on their birthday, or any other day, really. Sprinkle a little catnip and sing "Happy Birthday" to your favorite kitty!

Dibble's Kitty Cat Birthday Cake

Serves 1

Coconut or olive oil

1 (5-ounce) can of tuna in water, drained

¼ cup cooked, shredded plain chicken breast

1 large egg

1 tablespoon oat or rice flour

A few sprinkles of dried catnip (optional)

1 Preheat the oven to 350°F. Grease a 6- or 8-ounce ramekin or one cavity of a 12-cup muffin tin with oil and set aside.

2 Mash the tuna and chicken together in a small bowl until well combined. Add the egg and mix thoroughly. Mix in the oat flour to bind everything together.

3 Spoon the mixture into the prepared ramekin and press down. Bake for 10 to 12 minutes or until the cake is firm and slightly golden. Let cool completely. To serve, invert the cake into your kitty's bowl and sprinkle with catnip, if using.

Whether you have a tattooed golden retriever, a dog dyed Key lime green, a pup named Kitty, or any other kind of doggy companion, this recipe will definitely have them begging at your feet. Sing "Happy Birthday" to your best boy or girl and enjoy watching them lick their plate clean.

Good Boy Birthday Cake

Serves 2 to 4 (but let's face it, your pup could eat the whole thing)

Coconut or olive oil
1 cup oat flour
½ teaspoon baking soda
¼ cup unsalted creamy peanut butter
¼ cup coconut oil
½ cup applesauce or pumpkin puree
1 large egg
1 ripe banana, mashed

FROSTING
¼ cup plain whole milk Greek yogurt
1 tablespoon unsalted creamy peanut butter

1 Preheat the oven to 350°F. Grease a 6-inch cake pan or the wells of a muffin tin with oil. Set aside.

2 Whisk together the flour and baking soda in a medium bowl.

3 In a separate medium bowl, stir together the peanut butter, oil, applesauce, egg, and mashed banana until smooth.

4 Add the dry ingredients to the wet mixture and stir until well combined. Pour the batter into the prepared pan or divide among the wells of the tin.

5 Bake until golden brown and a toothpick inserted into the center comes out clean, 20 to 25 minutes if baking in a cake pan, or 10 to 12 minutes if baking in a muffin tin. Set aside and let completely cool.

6 **Meanwhile make the frosting:** Mix together the Greek yogurt and peanut butter in a small bowl until smooth. Spread it over the cooled cake or cupcakes and serve up a size/amount appropriate for your pup.

ACKNOWLEDGMENTS

There ain't no "I" in "team" and this book came together thanks to my band of A-Team members.

Extra-special friendship bracelets go to:

Stephanie: Thank you for always being open to my hundreds of wild ideas and moving on this one with the speed of lightning on your feet!

Emma: You championed this project from the very beginning and gave a small-town Pennsylvania girl this opportunity. Thank you for trusting me to bring this to fruition. (With a million Easter eggs and all!)

Kristen: Thank you not only for making my favorite pastries that look like dresses (and other styles), but also for writing the recipes for this book.

Jak aka Shibby: I had so much fun fighting lighting with you. Thank you for the dazzling photos and the memories we made along the way.

Sophia: There might have been glitter on the floor after the photo shoots, but it was worth it for how you made each recipe shimmer. Thank you for ensuring every item looked gorgeous.

Eva: We learned about this book deal at the Eras Tour in Vienna (RIP) and we got to celebrate together at the Eras Tour in Toronto. I know we'll be playing back a thousand of our memories for years to come.

Arial: Thanks for always meeting me in the pouring rain—whether it's in Foxborough at the Eras Tour or when I needed help ensuring the playlists in this book were perfect. Thanks for being my ride-or-die Swiftie.

Jenna: Thank you for being a good neighbor and bringing me props very swiftly.

Keisha: Thank you for lending me a hand—literally. You are a hand model SuperStar.

Tai: Thank you for bringing your magical creative self to this project and ensuring the cover and pages in this book stay beautiful.

Jude and Rachel: Thank you for being as detailed with editing as Taylor is with her album releases!

Special thanks to my best friend, Zach: While you did absolutely nothing for this project, you are my emotional support throughout life and you did manage to score us Eras Tour tickets for Pittsburgh Night 2.

Derek: You are the best thing that's ever been mine.

Last, but not least, the Swifties: This book would not exist without you, so thank you for making my wildest dreams come true. From online fan accounts to friends I've met at shows—thank you for bringing your all to this fandom and making sure everyone at the table feels included.

EASTER EGG KEY

This entire book is sprinkled with Easter eggs.

In the recipe introductions and throughout the text, you will find lots of Swiftie-verse references, including puns on lyrics, mentions of very specific dates, and even some of Taylor's nicknames. Since there are too many to list in the key here, we encourage you to highlight all the references you can find throughout the book and see how many you come up with.

When it comes to the photos, there is at least one Easter egg, ranging from very easy (like a nod to the recipe itself) to extra hard (like props from music videos that only eagle-eyed Swifties might notice).

Try to find them all and cross-reference the key below to test your Swiftie knowledge.

BREAKFAST AT MIDNIGHTS

Cruller Summer with Lavender Glaze: The orange arrows and purple glitter are a nod to the orange arrow and purple glitter featured in the "Anti-Hero" music video when Taylor gets struck in the heart with the arrow. The heart sunglasses are a nod to the "22" music video.

A Victory Pop(Star)-Tart in This World: The tarts themselves are decorated to reflect both a friendship bracelet and the "bejeweled" outfit in the music video. The friendship bracelet features the initials "TS," and it includes exactly thirteen candy "beads."

Fortnight Cinnamon Rolls: The teapot in this photo is meant to mimic the teapot seen in Taylor's "Fortnight" YouTube short challenge. The Quill Pen is a nod to the general lyric theme of *The Tortured Poets Department*. Last, the word "Florida" can be seen lightly in the book pages as a hat tip to the song "Florida!!!"

Drivin' a New Maserati Biscotti: There are mirrorballs and a cat in the background of this photo, but the real star is the coffee mug. This mug is a nod to the coffee mug the dad was drinking out of in "All Too Well: The Short Film," during the scene where they are all sitting around the dining room.

I Rose Up from the Banana Bread: The slice of banana is shaped into a snake and the parchment paper is mimicked after the Reputation Stadium Tour confetti.

KARMA IS A COOKIE

Cowboy (Cookie) Like Me: The milk is in a cowboy boot–shaped cup and there is a guitar pick on the tray.

15-Minute No-Bake Cookies: The chalkboard platter is a nod to the chalkboard featured in the "Fifteen" music video. Additionally, there are glitter gel pens, dice that add up to thirteen, and a King of Hearts card as a nod to "King of My Heart," and the ace is a nod to a lyric in "New Romantics."

There Is an Indentation Thumbprint Cookie: The gold leaf on one of the cookies represents the "golden tattoo" lyric from "Dress."

Invisible Locket Shaker Cookie: The sprinkles in these cookies include hearts, stars, music notes, microphones, mirrorballs, and "TS" initials.

Black-and-White Cookies with Screaming Color Sprinkles: This is meant to mimic a photo processing as a nod to the *1989* era with Polaroid photos.

Chai Cookies à la Taylor: One of the cookies has extra cinnamon on it as a hat tip to one of Taylor's Tumblr posts about fall where she said, "and baking your first batch of cookies but you put too much cinnamon in it because you're TOO EXCITED BECAUSE IT'S FALL."

So Scarlet, It Was Macaron: Not only are the macarons bejeweled to pay homage to the "bejeweled" music video, but the heart-shaped glass bowl is the same one seen in the "You Need to Calm Down" music video.

I BET YOU THINK ABOUT CAKE

Seven Bars of Chocolate Brownie and Blondie(s): The birthday hat is a miniature version of a hat Taylor wore for her birthday during the *Fearless* era. Also, choosing to feature the blondie in the middle of the photo is a nod to her being the best thing at the party.

I Bet You Think About Me Cupcakes: The table skirt and cupcake pay homage to the cake and table skirt in the "I Bet You Think About Me" music video.

Pennsylvania Under Me Whoopie Pies: This one is slightly more obvious with mirrorballs and stars. The treats are covered up on a mirror platter as a salute to a lyric in "Anti-Hero."

Blank Cake for a Big Cake, Happy Birthday: The cake itself mimics Taylor's birthday cake from her thirty-fourth birthday and the "Birthday Girl" tiara is one she wore for her birthday when she turned "thirtay."

Lover Cupcakes: The cupcake wrapper and the cotton candy represent the colors of the "Lover" album.

When You Think Tim McGraw Cake Cones: The cowboy hat pays homage to Taylor's debut record, *Taylor Swift*, when she rocked cowboy hats and cowboy boots.

PIE, PIE, BABY!

Cherry Pie with Crystal Skies: The clouds on the pie pay homage to the lyrics in "Blank Space," and the red-heart glasses give a nod to "22."

Bad Blood (Orange) Tart: The swords give a nod to weapons featured in the "Bad Blood" music video.

It's 2 a.m. Pie in a Jar: The names featured on the jars are the names of the three teenagers in a love triangle that Taylor described in the "folklore: The Long Pond Studio Sessions."

I Lived in Your Chess Pie: The chessboard is a nod to the song "Dear John." However, the chess pies have chess pieces on them that form a checkmate on the board, something that Taylor's dancers also do in the Eras Tour routine for the song "Mastermind."

The Smallest Pecan Pie Who Ever Lived: The red glove was featured in the "I Bet You Think About Me" music video. The push pin being stabbed into the pecan pie is a lyrical reference from "The Smallest Man Who Ever Lived."

You Need to Calm Down Pool Cups: These treats visually mimic the pool scene in the "You Need to Calm Down" music video where Taylor is sitting in an innertube float in a clear blue pool. The gummy bear even has a little pink jacket, similar to the one Taylor is wearing.

PASTRIES THAT LOOK LIKE DRESSES

Meet Me Behind the Mall Pretzel: The tissue paper mimics the Reputation Stadium tour confetti and the ring is a snake, both from the *Reputation* era.

Illicit Éclair: Each pastry was designed with something specific in mind, including the floral dress Taylor wore at the 2021 Grammys, the Eras Tour piano, "Lavender Haze" song, and the *Lover* album. Additionally, the necklace represents Taylor's initials on a chain around her neck, a slight nod at the lyrics from "Call It What You Want."

Chasing Churros in the Grocery Line: The cardigan sleeve seen in this shot is the original cardigan from the *folklore* era. There is also a friendship bracelet.

My Pain au Chocolat Fits in the Palm of Your Freezing Hand: The cardigan here is the official *Speak Now* cardigan.

I Can Make It with a Broken Heart Crispy Rice Pops: The friendship bracelets and the nod to the "broken heart" in the decorations.

Everybody Loves Pretty Pavlova: The pavlova itself is meant to represent the pavlova that Ina Garten and Taylor made. The addition of the florals alludes to the floral references Taylor uses both in her lyrics and in her art.

JUNIOR JEWELS

Junior Jewels Friendship Bracelets: The cafeteria trays in the background point to Taylor's high school years, when many of her early songs were written. The tray itself features a treasure trove of Easter eggs including friendship bracelets, a "T" keychain, the number "13," a cat marshmallow, and mirrorballs.

Fudge the Patriarchy: It's a clock, set at 12:13, which also happens to be Taylor's birthday. Additionally, the gold gear holding the clock hands together mimics ones seen in the "bejeweled" music video.

Vending Machine Cookie Dough Bites: The porcelain cat (wrapped around ivy) was featured in the "You Need to Calm Down" music video. Plus, the friendship bracelets, mirrorballs, and the "T" keychain. The clouds on the cookie dough bites represent the vibes of *1989*.

And All the Chocolate Pieces Fall Right into Place Bark: The guitar spoon and the guitar pick in the bowl both represent Taylor's musicianship.

Rep Going Down Popcorn: There are sprinkles scattered that spell out "REP TV," to represent *Reputation (Taylor's Version)*.

Midnight Lover Shake, Shake, Shake: While the shake color itself represents the *Lover* album with the pinks and blues, the sprinkles offer a *1989* vibe with the white clouds. To top it off, the cotton candy cloud mimics the clouds the dancers used during the "Lavender Haze" set on the Eras Tour.

Yes, I Got Your Letter (Candy): The fountain pen represents one of the three types of songs Taylor categorizes her songs in: Quill Lyrics, Fountain Pen Lyrics, and Glitter Gel Pen Lyrics. There are also bottles with candy "letters" in them to represent the song "Message in a Bottle." The red lips are a hat-tip to Taylor's classic red lip. And lastly, the white and pink candies are called "Squashies," which are Taylor's favorite U.K. candy.

Mirrorball Marshmallows: The ultimate mirrorball to give a shout-out to the song "mirrorball."

UNIVERSAL CONVERSION CHART

OVEN TEMPERATURE EQUIVALENTS

250°F = 120°C

275°F = 135°C

300°F = 150°C

325°F = 160°C

350°F = 180°C

375°F = 190°C

400°F = 200°C

425°F = 220°C

450°F = 230°C

475°F = 240°C

500°F = 260°C

MEASUREMENT EQUIVALENTS
Measurements should always be level unless directed otherwise.

⅛ teaspoon = 0.5 mL

¼ teaspoon = 1 mL

½ teaspoon = 2 mL

1 teaspoon = 5 mL

1 tablespoon = 3 teaspoons = ½ fluid ounce = 15 mL

2 tablespoons = ⅛ cup = 1 fluid ounce = 30 mL

4 tablespoons = ¼ cup = 2 fluid ounces = 60 mL

5⅓ tablespoons = ⅓ cup = 3 fluid ounces = 80 mL

8 tablespoons = ½ cup = 4 fluid ounces = 120 mL

10⅔ tablespoons = ⅔ cup = 5 fluid ounces = 160 mL

12 tablespoons = ¾ cup = 6 fluid ounces = 180 mL

16 tablespoons = 1 cup = 8 fluid ounces = 240 mL

INDEX

Note: Page references in *italics* indicate photographs.

A

Almond butter
  Do You Really Want to Know What I Ate April 29?, 189
  15-Minute No-Bake Cookies, 63–65, *64*
  Vending Machine Cookie Dough Bites, *190,* 191
Almond flour
  I Rose Up from the (Banana) Bread, 50–52, *51*
  So Scarlet, It Was Macaron, 85–88, *87*
  Vending Machine Cookie Dough Bites, *190,* 191
Almonds
  And All the Chocolate Pieces Fall Right into Place Bark, 192, *193*
  And You'll Poke That Bear Claw, 161–62
Apple Pie, Rose Garden, 139–40
Arcade Ring Popsicles, 184

B

Baking
  basic tools, 6–7
  colorful add-ons, 9
  rules and tips, 4–5
  specialty items, 7–8
Baking sheets, 6
Banana(s)
  And All the Chocolate Pieces Fall Right into Place Bark, 192, *193*
  Bread, I Rose Up from the, 50–52, *51*
  Good Boy Birthday Cake, 205
Bark, And All the Chocolate Pieces Fall Right into Place, 192, *193*
Bars
  Blondie(s)!, *98,* 99–100
  Cereal, You're on Your Own, Kid, 37
  Seven Bars of Chocolate Brownie, 96–98, *97*
Bear Claw, And You'll Poke That, 161–62
Berries
  Bad Blood (Orange) Tart, 131–33, *132*
  Daisy May's Strawberry Pretzel Salad, 144–45
  Everybody Loves Pretty Pavlova, 173–75, *174*
  It's 2 a.m. Pie in a Jar, 136–38, *137*
  Junior Jewels Candy Friendship Bracelet, 182, *183*
  Never Seen That Color (Blue)berry Cobbler, 134–35
  So Scarlet, It Was Macaron, 85–88, *87*
Biscotti, Drivin' a New Maserati, 47–49, *48*
Blondie(s)!, *98,* 99–100
Blueberries
  Bad Blood (Orange) Tart, 131–33, *132*
  Everybody Loves Pretty Pavlova, 173–75, *174*
  It's 2 a.m. Pie in a Jar, 136–38, *137*
  Never Seen That Color (Blue)berry Cobbler, 134–35
Bread, (Banana), I Rose Up from the, 50–52, *51*
Brownie, Seven Bars of Chocolate, 96–98, *97*
Buckeyes, You're My Best Friend, 194–95
Buckwheat Chocolate Chip Cookie (10-Minute Version), 91–93, *92*
Bundt cake pan, 8
Buttercream Frosting, Miss Americana, 26, *103*

C

Cake Cones, When You Think Tim McGraw, 119–20, *121*
Cake pans, 7
Cakes
  Blank, for a Big Cake, Happy Birthday, 110–12, *111*
  Coffee, at Midnight, 56–57
  Dibble's Kitty Cat Birthday, 204
  Good Boy Birthday, 205
  I Bet You Think About Cupcakes, 101–2, *103*
  Lover Cupcakes, 104–6, *105*
  Pennsylvania Under Me Whoopie Pies, 107–9, *108*
  On a Six-Lane Texas Sheet Pan, 117–18
  Welcome to New York Cheesecake, 113–14

Candy
    And All the Chocolate Pieces Fall Right into Place Bark, 192, *193*
    Fudge the Patriarchy, 185–86, *187*
    I'll Keep Your Peanut Brittle Heart Warm, 188
    Mirrorball Marshmallows, 202–3, *203*
    Yes, I Got Your Letter (with Candy!), *200*, 201
    You're My Best Friend Buckeyes, 194–95
Candy Friendship Bracelet, Junior Jewels, 182, *183*
Candy melts, 9
Candy thermometer, 8
Cereal
    Bars, You're on Your Own, Kid, 37
    I Can Make It with a Broken Heart Crispy Rice Pops, 176–78, *177*
Chai Cookies à la Taylor, 82–84, *83*
Cheese. *See* Cream Cheese; Mascarpone
Cheesecake, Welcome to New York, 113–14
Cherry Pie with Crystal Skies, 126–28, *127*
Chess Pie Bites, I Lived in Your, 141–42, *143*
Chicken
    Dibble's Kitty Cat Birthday Cake, 204

Chocolate
    Black-and-White Cookies with Screaming Color Sprinkles, 79–81, *80*
    Brownie, Seven Bars of, 96–98, *97*
    Chip Buckwheat Cookie (10-Minute Version), 91–93, *92*
    Cowboy (Cookies) Like Me, 60–62, *61*
    Do You Really Want to Know What I Ate April 29?, 189
    15-Minute No-Bake Cookies, 63–65, *64*
    Fudge the Patriarchy, 185–86, *187*
    I Bet You Think About Cupcakes, 101–2, *103*
    Illicit Éclairs, 163–65, *164*
    Mirrorball Marshmallows, 202–3, *203*
    My Pain au Chocolat Fits in the Palm of Your Freezing Hand, 168–70, *169*
    Pennsylvania Under Me Whoopie Pies, 107–9, *108*
    Pieces, And All the, Fall Right into Place Bark, 192, *193*
    Rep Going Down Popcorn, *196*, 197
    On a Six-Lane Texas Sheet Pan Cake, 117–18
    Three Months in the Grave Cups, 149–50, *150*
    You're My Best Friend Buckeyes, 194–95
Choux Dough, 29

Churros, Chasing, in the Grocery Line, 166, *167*
Cinnamon
    Bend When You Can, Gingersnap When You Have To, 89–90
    Chai Cookies à la Taylor, 82–84, *83*
    Chasing Churros in the Grocery Line, 166, *167*
    Rolls, Fortnight, *42*, 43–46
    Roll Sugar, 45
    Rose Garden Apple Pie, 139–40
Cobbler, Never Seen That Color (Blue)berry, 134–35
Coconut
    And All the Chocolate Pieces Fall Right into Place Bark, 192, *193*
    Blondie(s)!, *98*, 99–100
    Cowboy (Cookies) Like Me, 60–62, *61*
Coffee
    New Money, Tiramisu(it), and Tie, 115–16
Coffee (Cake) at Midnight, 56–57
Cookie Dough Bites, Vending Machine, *190*, 191
Cookies
    Bend When You Can, Gingersnap When You Have To, 89–90
    Buckwheat Chocolate Chip (10-Minute Version), 91–93, *92*
    Chai, à la Taylor, 82–84, *83*
    Cowboy, Like Me, 60–62, *61*

Crinkling (Eye) Lemon
  Drops, 68–69
Drivin' a New Maserati
  Biscotti, 47–49, *48*
15-Minute No-Bake, 63–65,
  64
Invisible Locket Shaker,
  75–78, *76*
Snow(balls) on the
  Beach, 70–71
Sugar, Christmas Tree
  Farm, 66–67
There Is an Indentation
  Thumbprint, 72–74, *73*
Cookie scoops, 8
Cotton candy
  Lover Cupcakes, 104–6,
    105
  Midnight Lover Shake, Shake,
    Shake!, *198,* 199
Cowboy (Cookies) Like Me,
  60–62, *61*
Cream Cheese
  The Best Day(nish), 156–57
  Daisy May's Strawberry
    Pretzel Salad, 144–45
  Frosting, 45
  Welcome to New York
    Cheesecake, 113–14
Crispy Rice Pops, I Can Make
  It with a Broken Heart,
  176–78, *177*
Cruller Summer with Lavender
  Glaze, 34–36, *35*
Cupcakes
  I Bet You Think About,
    101–2, *103*
  Lover, 104–6, *105*

D

Dates
  Do You Really Want to Know
    What I Ate April 29?, 189
Day(nish), The Best, 156–57
Doughs
  Choux, 29
  Pastry, 30
  Pie, Pie, Baby, 27
  Tart, The Best, 28

E

Easter eggs (secret messages),
  10, 207–9
Éclairs, Illicit, 163–65, *164*
Edible glitter, 9
Edible pens and writing gel, 9

F

Food dyes, 9
Food processor, 7
Friendship Bracelet, Junior
  Jewels Candy, 182, *183*
Frostings
  Buttercream, Miss Americana,
    26, *103*
  Cream Cheese, 45
Fruit. *See also* Berries;
  specific fruits
  The Best Day(nish), 156–57
  Junior Jewels Candy
    Friendship Bracelet, 182, *183*
Fudge the Patriarchy, 185–86, *187*

G

Gelatin
  You Need to Calm Down Pool
    Cups, *152,* 153

Ginger
  Autumn Leaves Falling Down
    Like Pieces of Pumpkin
    Pie, 129–30
  Bend When You Can,
    Gingersnap When You Have
    To, 89–90
Glaze, The Delicate, 25
Good Boy Birthday Cake, 205
Graham cracker crumbs
  It's 2 a.m. Pie in a Jar,
    136–38, *137*
  Rebekah's Key Lime
    Pie, 124–25
  Welcome to New York
    Cheesecake, 113–14

H

Hand mixer, 7

I

Ice cream
  Midnight Lover Shake, Shake,
    Shake!, *198,* 199
Isomalt, 9

K

Key Lime Pie, Rebekah's,
  124–25
Kitty Cat Birthday Cake,
  Dibble's, 204

L

Ladyfingers
  New Money, Tiramisu(it), and
    Tie, 115–16
Lavender Glaze, Cruller Summer
  with, 34–36, *35*
Lemon Drops, Crinkling
  (Eye), 68–69

Index

213

Lime, Key, Pie, Rebekah's, 124–25
Loaf pans, 7

M

Macaron, So Scarlet, It Was, 85–88, *87*
Madeleine mold, 8
Madeleines, Chloe or Sam or Sophia, 171–72
Marshmallows
    I Can Make It with a Broken Heart Crispy Rice Pops, 176–78, *177*
    Junior Jewels Candy Friendship Bracelet, 182, *183*
    Mirrorball, 202–3, *203*
Mascarpone
    New Money, Tiramisu(it), and Tie, 115–16
Measuring cups and spoons, 6
Mixing bowls, 6
Muffin tins, 7

N

Nut butter. *See also* Almond butter; Peanut butter
    You're on Your Own, Kid, Cereal Bars, 37
Nuts. *See also* Pecan(s)
    And All the Chocolate Pieces Fall Right into Place Bark, 192, *193*
    Blondie(s)!, *98,* 99–100
    Fudge the Patriarchy, 185–86, *187*
    I'll Keep Your Peanut Brittle Heart Warm, 188

Mirrorball Marshmallows, 202–3, *203*
And You'll Poke That Bear Claw, 161–62

O

Oats
    Cowboy (Cookies) Like Me, 60–62, *61*
    15-Minute No-Bake Cookies, 63–65, *64*
    Good Boy Birthday Cake, 205
Orange, Blood, Tart, Bad, 131–33, *132*

P

Pain au Chocolat, My, Fits in the Palm of Your Freezing Hand, 168–70, *169*
Parchment paper, 7
Par-Tays
    hosting, 10–11
    ideas for, 12–13
    playlists, 13–24
Pastries
    The Best Day(nish), 156–57
    Chasing Churros in the Grocery Line, 166, *167*
    Illicit Éclairs, 163–65, *164*
    My Pain au Chocolat Fits in the Palm of Your Freezing Hand, 168–70, *169*
    Victory Pop(Star)-Tarts, 38–41, *39*
    And You'll Poke That Bear Claw, 161–62
Pastry Dough, 30
Pavlova, Everybody Loves Pretty, 173–75, *174*

Peanut butter
    Good Boy Birthday Cake, 205
    Pennsylvania Under Me Whoopie Pies, 107–9, *108*
    Vending Machine Cookie Dough Bites, *190,* 191
    You're My Best Friend Buckeyes, 194–95
Peanut(s)
    And All the Chocolate Pieces Fall Right into Place Bark, 192, *193*
    Brittle Heart, I'll Keep Your, Warm, 188
Pecan(s)
    Cowboy (Cookies) Like Me, 60–62, *61*
    Pie, The Smallest Who Ever Lived, 146–48, *147*
    On a Six-Lane Texas Sheet Pan Cake, 117–18
    Snow(balls) on the Beach, 70–71
Pie, Pie, Baby Dough, 27
Pie dishes, 7
Pie(s)
    Apple, Rose Garden, 139–40
    Bites, Chess, I Lived in Your, 141–42, *143*
    Cherry, with Crystal Skies, 126–28, *127*
    Daisy May's Strawberry Pretzel Salad, 144–45
    in a Jar, It's 2 a.m., 136–38, *137*
    Key Lime, Rebekah's, 124–25
    Pecan, The Smallest Who Ever Lived, 146–48, *147*

Pumpkin, Autumn Leaves Falling Down Like Pieces of, 129–30
Piping bags and tips, 8
Popcorn, Rep Going Down, *196*, 197
Pops, Crispy Rice, I Can Make It with a Broken Heart, 176–78, *177*
Popsicle molds, 8
Popsicles, Arcade Ring, 184
Pop(Star)-Tarts, Victory, 38–41, *39*
Pretzel(s)
    And All the Chocolate Pieces Fall Right into Place Bark, 192, *193*
    Cowboy (Cookies) Like Me, 60–62, *61*
    Meet Me Behind the Mall, 158–60, *159*
    Strawberry Salad, Daisy May's, 144–45
Pudding
    Three Months in the Grave Cups, 149–50, *150*
Pumpkin
    Good Boy Birthday Cake, 205
    Pie, Autumn Leaves Falling Down Like Pieces of, 129–30
    Spice, Starbucks Lovers', 46

R

Raspberry jam
    There Is an Indentation Thumbprint Cookie, 72–74, *73*
Rolling pin, 7
Rolls, Fortnight Cinnamon, *42*, 43–46
Rose Garden Apple Pie, 139–40

S

Scones, Palace of, 53–55
Shake, Shake, Shake!, Midnight Lover, *198*, 199
Sifter, 7
Snow(balls) on the Beach, 70–71
Spatulas, 6
Spice grinder, 8
Springform pan, 8
Sprinkles, 9
    Blank Cake for a Big Cake, Happy Birthday, 110–12, *111*
    Invisible Locket Shaker Cookies, 75–78, *76*
    Mirrorball Marshmallows, 202–3, *203*
    Rep Going Down Popcorn, *196*, 197
    Screaming Color, Black-and-White Cookies with, 79–81, *80*
    Vending Machine Cookie Dough Bites, *190*, 191
    When You Think Tim McGraw Cake Cones, 119–20, *121*
    You Need to Calm Down Pool Cups, *152*, 153
Strawberry(ies)
    Everybody Loves Pretty Pavlova, 173–75, *174*
    Pretzel Salad, Daisy May's, 144–45
    So Scarlet, It Was Macaron, 85–88, *87*
Sugar, Cinnamon Roll, 45
Sugar Cookies, Christmas Tree Farm, 66–67

T

Tart Dough, The Best, 28
Tart pans, 8
Tarts
    Bad Blood (Orange), 131–33, *132*
    Victory Pop(Star)-, 38–41, *39*
Thumbprint Cookie, There Is an Indentation, 72–74, *73*
Tiramisu(it), New Money, and Tie, 115–16
Tuna
    Dibble's Kitty Cat Birthday Cake, 204

W

Walnuts
    Fudge the Patriarchy, 185–86, *187*
Whisk, 6
White chocolate
    Blondie(s)!, *98*, 99–100
    Cowboy (Cookies) Like Me, 60–62, *61*
    Mirrorball Marshmallows, 202–3, *203*
    Rep Going Down Popcorn, *196*, 197
    Seven Bars of Chocolate Brownie, 96–98, *97*
Whoopie Pies, Pennsylvania Under Me, 107–9, *108*
Wire cooling racks, 7
Wooden spoons, 6

LINDSEY SMITH is a publishing professional and bookseller and the award-winning author of several books, including *Eat Your Feelings*. She also writes gift products and is the cocreator of *Pup Talks* and *The Bibliophile Oracle Deck*. She has been featured in *O, The Oprah Magazine*; *PopSugar*; *Cosmopolitan*; *Parade* magazine; the *Chicago Tribune;* ABC; NBC; CBS; the *Today* show; TEDxPittsburgh, and other outlets. She recently opened a bookstore, One Idea Books and Gifts, in her hometown of Leechburg, Pennsylvania. She's an OG Swiftie and even worked at Taylor's perfume booth during the Red Tour.